SUPERMODELS DISCOVERED

SUPERMODELS DISCOVERED

CAROLINE LEAPER

LAURENCE KING

LAURENCE KING

First published in Great Britain in 2025 by
Laurence King
An imprint of Quercus Editions Ltd
Carmelite House
50 Victoria Embankment
London EC4Y 0DZ

An Hachette UK company

A CIP catalogue record for this book is available from the
British Library

HB ISBN 9781529433234

Ebook ISBN 9781529433241

10 9 8 7 6 5 4 3 2 1

Cover images from left to right and top to bottom:
Cindy Crawford; Janice Dickinson; Ashely Graham;
Pat Cleveland; Claudia Schiffer; Halima Aden;
Amber Valletta; Naomi Campbell; Gigi Hadid.

Frontispiece (page 2): Barbara Goalen with
photographer David Olius, 1953

Designer: Kieron Lewis
Commissioning editor: Sophie Wise
Project manager: Jessica Spencer
Picture researcher: Sophie Hartley

Printed and bound in China by C&C Offset Printing Co., Ltd.

TO CAMRON AND EVA

Anok Yai, Paco Rabanne Spring/Summer 2020.

INTRODUCTION

'How were you discovered?' It's the question that everyone wants to ask a supermodel. The response is usually a story that doesn't disappoint.

Plucked from obscurity or Instagram, privilege or poverty, all of the women featured in this book came from different circumstances and locations all over the globe to find themselves at the apex of glamour, working at the very top of the alluring, lucrative, controversial and competitive world of high fashion.

Some were scouted by chance at the airport or were out shopping with friends when they were spontaneously offered a life-changing opportunity. Others entered beauty contests, or signed up to etiquette classes and modelling schools to find their way in. These origin stories can read like rags-to-riches fairy tales, filled with plot twists, highs and lows. Certainly, you couldn't make them up.

Beyond the already exceptional chance of being approached by an agent, editor or photographer, the stars who have 'made it' experienced numerous false starts as well as breakthrough career moments. Hundreds of good models are signed and launched each year globally but very few manage to capture public attention and — crucially — keep it. Persistence and patience are common themes, as almost all faced repeated rejection before seeing any glimpse of success. →

Claudia Schiffer and Cindy Crawford, MTV Awards, 1991.

Most were incredibly young when they started out in the highly pressurized fashion industry. They had to navigate the adult world, encountering ruthless dealmakers and, at times, predatory behaviour. These were teenagers completing their first assignments in cities far from home, and not all were lucky enough to be chaperoned by parents or older siblings. They were driven by the promise of a fabulous life and, typically, a new-found passion for creating beautiful, captivating and provocative imagery.

The fashion industry is flawed and fickle, and throughout history has mirrored intolerance and closed-mindedness in the wider world. Racism, sizeism and ageism are present throughout these stories — even the most recent ones. But fashion can also be a catalyst — every new challenger with a seminal magazine cover appearance or a must-see catwalk turn can prove influential and usher in societal change. For better or worse, models can represent beauty ideals and set standards on everything from hair styles to body shapes.

The industry's relentless pursuit of newness can be particularly harsh for its models — one can define the look of the moment, but what about when that moment has passed? We've moved through eras favouring haughty elegance, then a 'youthquake', 'waifs' then 'Amazonians'. Typically, when a trending look peaks, designers and photographers seek a counterpoint, and the

pendulum swings in the opposite direction. If the best supermodels can symbolize an era, the very, very best can transcend several, their image and their output adapting with the times to stay relevant.

All the women featured in this book have reached the top, but the parameters of success and what warrants 'supermodel' status have changed drastically along the way. The term 'supermodel' was written in the media as early as 1891, but it is widely accepted that its first use in context was in 1942: journalist Judith Cass's *Chicago Tribune* headline read 'Super Models Are Signed for Fashion Show'. Being recognized as a supermodel has loosely, since then, required the claimant to bank a combination of prestigious catwalk appearances, artistic magazine editorials, glossy fashion advertising images and money-making beauty contracts. But, over time, and with globalization, new levels of fame and fandom have regularly reshaped the supposed criteria. Other coveted prizes may include a solo *Vogue* cover (a rarity since actresses began to claim cover spots in the mid 1990s) or reaching a certain number of followers on Instagram.

Super fans may argue that a true supermodel should have scored all of the big four *Vogue* covers — American, British, French and Italian — a superfecta that is almost impossible to achieve in the modern era of celebrity. Equally, those who may once have been considered supermodels on their home turf would perhaps not challenge the international household names who take the biggest pay cheques today. This media tattle — rich lists, follower counts and model of the year accolades — fuels the discourse around the supermodel enigma, and keeps our interest piqued from generation to generation.

Exactly how new models are being 'discovered' also reflects wider cultural shifts. For Jean Shrimpton, who launched her career in 1960, it was a case of graduating from etiquette classes at a London charm academy. Christy Turlington, in the late 1980s, carried a physical portfolio full of her photographs to catalogue castings all over Manhattan before she got her break, shooting with Arthur Elgort at *Vogue*. For Anok Yai, who was spotted at a homecoming weekend festival in 2017, it was a street-style photo posted on social media that caught the attention of an agent. Mere weeks later, she made headlines with a historic Prada catwalk booking.

The methods of discovery have evolved. Where once a designer or photographer may have introduced their particularly tall and beautiful high-society friend to a magazine editor they knew, now anyone, from anywhere, could potentially become a supermodel. After Kate Moss was spotted by chance at JFK airport, in 1988, and her story became world-famous, a model scout would never again leave home without a Polaroid camera or, later, a camera phone. Social media allows aspiring models to publish their 'portfolio' of sorts — there's no need to lug a physical book around. The new accessibility means that the stars who dominate today feel ever more reflective of real society — although there is always more to be done by all in the industry to push for greater diversity, inclusivity and representation. →

This book begins with the story of Lisa Fonssagrives, who launched her career in 1936 just as *Vogue* began to use colour photographs on its covers instead of illustrations. Working with Horst P. Horst and Irving Penn, she became an icon in the post-war couture boom. Through 52 more profiles, we progress to Adut Akech, born in Kenya's largest refugee camp and raised to stardom under the mentorship of the eminent *Vogue* editor Edward Enninful in 2017. For her, an average catwalk-show appearance is met with a barrage of camera phones, and her every image is devoured by a social media fanbase of millions.

The 53 individual profiles in *Supermodels Discovered* are ordered chronologically by the model's date of birth, making it easy to appreciate how advances in photography, technology, clothing production, advertising, feminism, social media, cosmetics and celebrity culture have all changed what it means to be a model over time.

Through original interviews exclusive to this book, we learn how Claudia Schiffer really felt when she was approached in a Düsseldorf discothèque, and why Karen Elson felt drawn to the fashion industry as a way to see the world beyond her hometown. Stephanie Seymour explains what prompted her to cut a coupon from a magazine and enter a modelling contest in 1984, while Janice Dickinson describes some of her early run-ins with the 20th century's greatest designers. Pat Cleveland mastered her signature walk while standing on a shaky table in 1966 - and Coco Rocha tells how, in 2006, she practised hers with a coach on a sweltering New York rooftop.

Halima Aden found fame overnight in 2016 when her beauty-pageant debut went viral on the internet — she describes how the industry 'craved authenticity' when she became the first hijab-wearing supermodel. Amber Valletta speaks of the 'girl band' sorority that the 1990s supermodels formed, to cope with the 'pressure cooker' they found themselves in. And Beverly Johnson explains that, when she became the first Black woman on the cover of American *Vogue* in 1974, her life went into 'hyperdrive'.

These insights are candid and colourful — memories of those pivotal moments are fresh in their minds, whether they took place five years ago, or fifty.

These are biographies filled with haute couture and drama, beauty and business savvy. Discover how some of the richest and most powerful women in the fashion world began their careers when given their one-in-a-million chance.

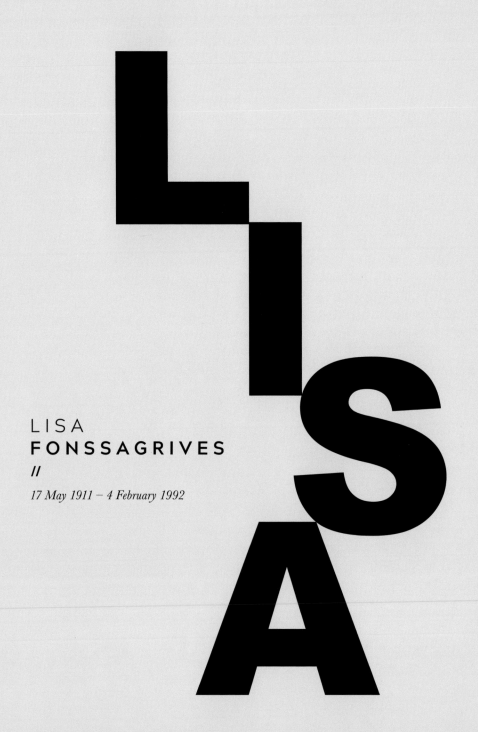

LISA
FONSSAGRIVES
//
17 May 1911 – 4 February 1992

If we define a 'supermodel' as the most in-demand, highly paid face of their era, then Lisa Fonssagrives was likely the first. Fashion photography was in its infancy when Lisa began her career in the mid-1930s – before then, magazines had relied on illustrations to depict the clothes designers were offering for the season.

Lisa Birgitta Bernstone was born in the relaxed Swedish town of Uddevalla. Her father was a dentist and her mother a nurse, but art was integral to family life. She practised painting, sculpture and dance, before leaving to study ballet at Berlin's Mary Wigman Schule when she was 20.

In 1933 she competed in Paris, fell in love with the city and decided to stay. She also met her first husband, French dancer Fernand Fonssagrives, and the couple started offering private dance classes to people in their own homes. When Fernand was injured, though, he picked up a Rolleiflex camera. Lisa naturally became his primary photography subject.

The pictures Fernand took of Lisa during the early days of their marriage were fearless and experimental for their time – she trusted his lens. Leaping across a St Tropez beach in her swimsuit, practising her elegant *grand jeté*, it was clear that, even with no modelling experience, Lisa knew how to move and sculpt her dancer's body for the camera.

In 1936, Lisa had what she would later recognize as her 'discovery' moment. She met the German photographer Willy Maywald in an elevator, and he asked if she might model some hats for him. Maywald worked as a house photographer shooting what we might now call lookbooks for Christian Dior and Jacques Fath. Lisa obliged.

Maywald's pictures were submitted to French *Vogue* and Horst P. Horst, who had recently joined as staff photographer, asked her to do some test shots. The day before her first official *Vogue* sitting a few months later, Lisa was briefed that she would model gowns by Alix and Lucien Lelong. She went straight to the Louvre to do her homework, studying how people posed, in evening clothes, in paintings and sculptures. →

Lisa had the foresight to think of fashion photography as a fine-art form, and the images she featured in during the late 1930s remain some of the most important and exciting in history. In 1939, she utilized her strength, balance and poise as a dancer as she waved her Lelong skirt perilously off the frame of the Eiffel Tower for Erwin Blumenfeld's lens. A health-and-safety officer would surely never sign that off on set today.

When World War II began, Lisa and Fernand emigrated to New York and she began working regularly for American *Vogue*. For her debut June 1940 cover, shot by Horst P. Horst, she twisted her body to spell out V-O-G-U-E, while wearing a blue-and-white Brigance bathing suit.

Demand for Lisa heightened as her neatly pointed nose and lofty expression appealed to the market of the moment. She became a role model for American women – a New York *Daily News* article from June 1940 described how women were copying her 'pompadour' hairstyle at home.

Lisa modelled for Bergdorf Goodman and Schiaparelli, *Town & Country* and *Harper's Bazaar*. For its May 1947 issue, American *Vogue* commissioned the first seminal portrait of its top models of the moment, '12 Beauties'. Photographer Irving Penn (whom she would later marry, in 1950, after divorcing her first husband) positioned Lisa at the centre of his composition.

'They represent an Omnibus of Beauty,' the magazine said of the 'the most photographed models in America'. They are a 'current replacement of Ziegfeld and Gibson Girl legends'.

Lisa was, by any standards, a supermodel by this point. She featured on the cover of *TIME* magazine in September 1949, fronting an article linking the booming business of modelling with the dawn of advertising. When most good models earned $10 to $25 an hour, Lisa was making $40.

'The model is an illusion that can sell evening gowns, nylons and refrigerators,' the article noted of her versatility, and the fact she was now recognizable in every household in America. 'She can sell diapers and cemetery plots.'

DORIAN

DORIAN **LEIGH**
//

23 April 1917 – 7 July 2008

Are you ever 'too old' to become a supermodel? Dorian Leigh was 27 when she arrived at Harry Conover's New York agency in 1944, with two children, one divorce and three career changes already to her name.

She might just have something, Conover told her, if she could convince the *Harper's Bazaar* fashion editor, Diana Vreeland, that she was only 19. Dorian met the next day with Vreeland and the photographer Louise Dahl-Wolfe, who were mesmerized by her peaked eyebrows. Her first assignment was the magazine's June 1944 cover, dressed as a 'summer bride' in a blush organza gown trimmed with copious ribbons and roses.

The plotline of Dorian's discovery somewhat mimicked the movie of the moment: Rita Hayworth's *Cover Girl*. Whether the reality was quite as serendipitous doesn't matter – as Leigh's sister Suzy Parker would later say in Eileen Ford's *Beauty Now and Forever* (1977), Dorian 'never looks back, and when she does … she writes her script the way she wants to write it.'

Dorian Leigh Parker was born in San Antonio, Texas, but enjoyed a privileged childhood in New York City. Her father invented a new etching acid, earning a fortune. She loved fashion from an early age and would take a seamstress with her to the cinema to sketch up the latest trends, straight from the screen.

She studied English at the private Randolph-Macon College, Virginia, married at 20, and had two children before divorcing. She moved back to Queens with her parents, and her father encouraged her to study calculus at New York University. When she graduated, she worked for the US Navy and designed wing components for the Eastern Aircraft Corporation during World War II.

After the war, she pursued copywriting at Republic Pictures, before trying her luck as a model with Conover. Success came fast: Dorian's versatility made her popular with the leading photographers of the time. When fashion photography generally felt static, she moved – leapt, pouted and flirted – for the camera. →

'In a room or at the theatre she can look small, nervous, often sullen,' Irving Penn said of his muse in the February 1947 issue of *Vogue*. 'Dorian Leigh's beauty is completely made for the camera.'

Dorian shot six covers of American *Vogue* in 1946, spanning a demure sitting with a fruit bowl by Horst P. Horst for April, to an enchanting Penn portrait for December, distracting actor Ray Bolger dressed as Santa. She was also featured in Penn's landmark '12 Beauties' in 1947.

Her work for *Vogue* and *Harper's*, French *Elle* and *Paris Match* was celebrated, but Dorian became a household name when she shook up the world of beauty advertising with Revlon. From around 1944 the brand began to promote its lipsticks and nail polishes via colour photo advertisements, replacing illustrations. Dorian's debut campaign was 1945's Fatal Apple ('the most tempting colour since Eve winked at Adam') but it was her risqué 1952 'Fire and Ice' pictures, shot by Richard Avedon, that made her a Madison Avenue advertising legend. She dramatically splayed her painted nails across her face, as the caption teased: 'For you who love to flirt with fire ... who dare to skate on thin ice ...'

The newspapers revelled in Dorian's personal life. She ultimately married and divorced five times, and had five children, describing herself as one of the first liberated women. Her 'happy-go-lucky' attitude was said to have inspired her friend, author Truman Capote, when writing the character of Holly Golightly in *Breakfast at Tiffany's*.

In 1956, she moved to Paris and founded her own model agency, The Fashion Bureau, with an innovative voucher system to ensure models were paid promptly for their work. She encouraged her teenage sister, Suzy Parker, to follow in her footsteps and sign with Eileen Ford. Parker's fame would eventually eclipse Dorian's, as she found more success in acting.

'When I was at the peak of my success as a model, I did feel I had everything,' Dorian wrote in her 1980 autobiography titled *The Girl Who Had Everything*. 'I wore the most beautiful clothes, was photographed by the world's greatest photographers, travelled all over the world, had all the money I needed, was pursued by men whose names were household words ... who could ask for anything more?'

The Ambassador Magazine, 1952, photographer Elsbeth Juda.

BARBARA

BARBARA
GOALEN
//

1 January 1921 – 16 June 2002

British models were known as mannequins until the early 1950s when the term 'model' came across from America. Barbara Goalen, therefore, could be considered the inaugural 'super mannequin' – she was one of the first exports from London to gain employment with Paris's couturiers.

Until 1947, she was a settled British housewife with no intention of becoming a model. But when her pilot husband was killed in a plane crash, she decided to follow a friend's advice and give it a try.

She didn't need to work for the money, and acknowledged the pursuit was entirely for her self-confidence. She had worked previously as a cartographist for the British Overseas Airways Corporation at Whitechurch during the war. But her father was a rubber plantation owner in Malaysia, and her childhood had been privileged.

When she began commuting to London for modelling test shoots, her parents helped to raise her two children back in Hampshire. She had previously met Giuseppe Mattli – who was then one of the city's 'big ten' designers – at a party and contacted him to ask for some work.

Mattli gave her a six-month contract as a house model. It was a Mattli picture published in the *Daily Express* that then got her noticed by another designer, Julian Rose. By 1948, she had appeared in British *Vogue* and *Harper's Bazaar*, photographed by John French, Richard Dormer and John Deakin. She made her debut in Paris that summer, posing for Clifford Coffin's lens at Christian Dior.

Her tiny waist appealed to Cristóbal Balenciaga and Dior, whose pioneering New Look had just launched. Barbara had the couture look, just at the time it was being defined. →

Her international popularity only boosted her fame back at home – her haughty eyebrows arched across billboard advertisements on London Underground stations, as well as making it onto the silver screen – she had film parts in *Elizabeth of Ladymead* (1948) and *Maytime in Mayfair* (1949). She featured in almost every issue of both British *Vogue* and *Harper's Bazaar* in 1950 and earned £3,000 per year at a time when £300 was considered a good annual salary in London.

Barbara's success was peaking, but she was one of the first supermodels to realize the value of exclusivity and decided to take control of her career. Her face had become 'as familiar to Britons as Winston Churchill's', according to a *Herald Sun* story in February 1951. The article detailed how Barbara took a few weeks off to have cosmetic surgery on the tip of her nose, and at the same time decided to up her fees and reduce her appearances in order to keep her edge. 'She mustn't be too scarce though, or she'd be forgotten,' the story noted. 'Nor must she be seen too often, or there'll be demand for someone new.'

She became selective about which photographers she would work with, and produced some of the most important photos of her career, modelling wasp-waisted Balenciaga and Cartier diamond brooches for Deakin and Anthony Denney at *Vogue*.

She worked with British photographers to utilize unexpected locations as backdrops – Lancashire's cotton mills with Elsbeth Juda, or the platform at Green Park Station with French.

She also represented the British fashion trade abroad – in January 1952 she embarked on a month-long tour of America, Australia and New Zealand, showcasing designs for debutantes by Miki Sekers and the West Cumberland Silk Mills. *The Sunday Times Magazine* named her a Person of the Year.

In February 1954, aged 33, she remarried. Barbara had only been a model for six years, but by the July she had retired. She devoted herself to her new family life and had two more children. She worked occasionally in film, organized charity events and debutante balls and wrote a few fashion-advice stories for *The Daily Telegraph*. Her old modelling photographs, notably, were relegated to a box in her basement.

DOVIMA

Dovima was the first mononymous supermodel, but her brand name wasn't a marketing stunt conceived by a strategic agent.

Born Dorothy Virginia Margaret Juba in Jackson Heights, Queens, New York City, she combined the initials of her given names as a child. Between the ages of 10 and 17, Dorothy was housebound due to rheumatic fever and was home-schooled. For want of contact with children her own age, she invented Dovima as an imaginary friend.

Her first published portrait was taken at the age of two, holding a doll for the March 1929 issue of the *Benevolent Association Bulletin*. When she turned 17, she supported her parents, a Polish American policeman and his Irish American wife, initially by working as a waitress and in a sweet shop.

Dorothy married her childhood upstairs neighbour Jack Golden in 1948. Golden simply moved downstairs, into her bedroom at her parents' apartment.

The legend goes that the newlyweds dined at the Horn & Hardart fast-food Automat on Manhattan's 42nd Street, near the Graybar Building, which was then the home of Condé Nast's American magazines. As they left, an editor from *Vogue* spotted Dovima, and invited her inside to do a test shoot that afternoon and to shoot with Irving Penn the next day. The rest is history.

In reality, Dovima had been working with prominent photographers for at least a couple of years by that point. She clearly revelled in her serendipitous Irving Penn tale, though. 'I suppose you would like to hear the story of how I was discovered?' she teased in an August 1986 interview with the *Orlando Sentinel*. 'All the gossip columnists loved it.' →

Her significant early pictures had included a 1946 double-exposure fashion story by Gjon Mili for *LIFE* magazine, and a shoot in Jamaica with Toni Frissell, wearing a polka-dot Carolyn Schnurer bikini (the first bikini to be photographed outside France, according to Christie's). So, by 1949 when Dovima would recount her discovery, she was already an in-demand model.

Her career did accelerate in 1949, though. Richard Avedon photographed her for the May issue of *Harper's Bazaar*; in the summer she illustrated two 'what to buy in July' editorials for American *Vogue*, and in the September issue she starred in portraits by Irving Penn and Norman Parkinson.

The photographers were infatuated with her elegance and unattainability. Her lips remained pursed (apparently, to hide a chipped tooth) and the expression came to define a sophisticated photography style associated with 1950s couture. Dovima's poise and smirk saw her compared to the Mona Lisa. In July 1956, Avedon described her 'poetry of movement' in the *Richmond Times-Dispatch* of Virginia, 'No matter what pose she falls into, she is graceful,' he said.

By 1950, Dovima was signed to the Eileen Ford Agency. She became a muse to Avedon, he shot her in Egypt for *Harper's Bazaar*, comparing her beauty to the Queen Nefertiti. The shoot took place during his honeymoon with his second wife, and Dovima's second husband was also present – he would accompany her on all assignments, and famously brought a trunk full of comic books to keep her entertained.

At the peak of her career in the mid-1950s, it is estimated that Dovima completed over 500 editorial shoots. Her most famous picture, 'Dovima with Elephants', was lensed by Avedon for the September 1955 issue of *Harper's Bazaar*. When most fashion photographs were still taken in studios, Avedon captured his favourite beauty with two exotic beasts at the Cirque Medrano in Paris. Dovima wore the debut evening gown created by Yves Saint Laurent, who was then working as Christian Dior's assistant.

As London's 1960s 'youthquake' reached New York, though, Dovima could see that her image might fall out of fashion. In 1962, aged 35, she retired from modelling. 'I didn't want to wait until the camera turned cruel,' she would later say.

1962, photographer Jerry Schatzberg.

CHINA
MACHADO
//

25 December 1929 – 18 December 2016

C H I N A

China Machado's biography read like a movie script, even before she became a model at the age of 24.

She was born Noelie Machado and grew up in Shanghai's affluent French Concession in the 1930s. Her father was Portuguese and from Macau, while her mother was from Hong Kong. She spoke seven languages at home, including Portuguese, French, English and Chinese. When she was six, she survived typhoid and meningitis. Her hospital was attacked during a Japanese invasion – she was presumed dead and placed on a lorry full of bodies before her father came to find her.

The family fled the Japanese occupation when she was 16 and they travelled to Spain, then Argentina. At 19, she became a Pan Am flight attendant and lived with her brother in Peru. It was here that she met the most famous bullfighter in the world, Luis Miguel Dominguin. Three days later, they eloped to Rome and married, much to the shock of her family.

China's life with Dominguin was fabulous – she found herself at the centre of a social set with Pablo Picasso and Errol Flynn, and travelled the world. But when Dominguin left her for the Hollywood starlet Ava Gardner, it was time for China's own second act.

In 1954 she moved to Paris, alone, as she had some friends in the city. She changed her name to China (pronounced Chee-na) at this time. One of those friends took her to a cocktail party, where she was asked if she wanted to model for Balenciaga. She went to meet with Balenciaga, but the meeting was cancelled because he was out of town. The team sent her to see Hubert de Givenchy instead.

'They thought I was filling in for a sick girl,' she recalled in a 2014 interview with website Into the Gloss. 'I barely knew anything about walking like a model, so I just copied the girl in front of me. At the end of the show, gorgeous Givenchy comes up to me and says, "Would you like to be in the *cabine*?" That's how it all started.' →

China joined Givenchy's *cabine* for three years – the group of model muses who worked with his house exclusively. Later, she would model for Dior and Balenciaga too, becoming the highest-paid catwalk model of her time in Europe, commanding $1,000 per day.

Until that point, China was a walker, not a press model – she was styled for intimate couture presentations but had gained little experience as a photographic muse. That all changed when she went to America in 1958. The designer Oleg Cassini had seen her in Paris and first invited her to model in his catwalk shows in New York, on a contract.

China accepted and moved to the United States. On arrival, she met *Harper's Bazaar* editor Diana Vreeland, who within days asked her to model some striking, hot-pink Balenciaga pyjamas in a catwalk show she was hosting at the Waldorf Astoria.

And that's where Richard Avedon, the *Bazaar* photographer, first saw her. China became Avedon's latest favoured subject – he photographed her couture gowns and exotic furs, her poise and elegance evident in every image. Yet, initially, *Bazaar* wouldn't run the pictures.

Avedon protested and campaigned against the publishing directors at the time, threatening to quit his contract in support of China. Finally, they relented – China became the first non-white model to ever feature inside any leading American fashion magazine, in the February 1959 issue.

China continued working in front of Avedon's lens before, in 1962, he and Vreeland offered her the opportunity to get behind it. She became the fashion director of *Harper's Bazaar*, styling shoots with Elizabeth Taylor and Judy Garland. Her life had taken yet another glamorous turn.

CARMEN DELL'OREFICE
//
3 June 1931

Carmen Dell'Orefice's debut shoot was 'a big flop'. Aged just 13, she was on the bus to her ballet class when the wife of photographer Herman Landschoff asked her if she had ever considered modelling.

A test shoot was set up for *Harper's Bazaar* at Jones Beach, Long Island. Afterwards, the magazine wrote to Carmen's mother to say they couldn't use the pictures. 'They said I was unphotogenic,' she would later tell the *Los Angeles Times*.

Two years later, she got another chance when a family friend introduced her to Cecil Beaton – the photographer worked for American *Vogue*. Within weeks she was on a $7.50-an-hour contract with the magazine, and had posed for Beaton, Horst P. Horst and Irving Penn. The results were mostly published in the July 1946 issue.

Carmen had arrived – but she was still only a teenager navigating the adult world of fashion photography. She posed nude for Salvador Dalí, who paid her $7 for the sitting and gave her a painting to keep. Erwin Blumenfeld shot her first *Vogue* cover for the October 1947 issue; her delicate shoulders were draped in pink silk satin and jewel brooches clipped back her hair. The cover line called her 'A New Kind of Beauty'.

Although she now had some money, Carmen's income wasn't enough to support the Dell'Orefice household. She described her upbringing as 'penniless and hungry' in an interview with the *Daily Mail*. She overcame an unstable home life with her Italian father and Hungarian mother. A bout of rheumatic fever stopped her ballet career, just as she was offered a scholarship to the Ballets Russes. Swimming was prescribed to ease the symptoms – she excelled at it, but broke a leg before the tryouts for the 1952 Olympics. →

American *Vogue*, August 1946, photographer Constantin Joffe.

" THEY SAID I WAS UNPHOTOGENIC. "

Carmen and her mother both took on sewing projects on the side – one of their customers was Dorian Leigh, whose sister Suzy Parker later became best friends with Carmen. The household didn't have a telephone, and *Vogue* would send runners to their apartment to tell her when she was needed for a job.

In 1953, Eileen Ford signed Carmen. Work became steady and spanned both editorial and commercial clients. She toured America and Australia, presenting collections for Neiman Marcus, and fronted adverts for brands including Sears, Maidenform bras, Western Union financial services and Helena Rubinstein's blue-rinse hair dye.

In 1959 she began her second marriage, to photographer Richard Heimann. She retired from modelling – shooting almost nothing until 1978. It was then, at the age of 47, that Carmen said she really understood the fashion industry and felt like herself in photographs.

Her supermodel status, in fact, was sealed by her career renaissance. When her hair turned to a white sweep, her high cheekbones and elegant poses reminded clients of a bygone glamorous era.

'I wasn't full of personality, I was full of solitude and solemnity,' she told the *Daily Mail* in 2013, of her younger years in the industry. 'I wasn't a cover-girl type. I've had more covers in the past 15 years than I had in all the years before that.'

Carmen became the oldest supermodel still working, well into her 80s. For her, it was playing the long game that ultimately paid off.

American *Vogue*, January 1962, photographer Karen Radkai.

WILHELMINA
COOPER

//

1 May 1939 – 1 March 1980

At a time when a model's success might be measured solely by the number of covers they had graced, Wilhelmina Cooper reigned supreme. Her portraits fronted an estimated 218 different magazines, including 17 issues of American *Vogue* between 1962 and 1965. She was prolific and versatile: she snuggles a kitten and wears a chunky David Webb cuff on her *Vogue* debut; her eyelashes flutter from inside a jewelled birdcage for her finale.

She was a supermodel, but also in her legacy is her namesake agency and the thousands of other models whose careers she launched. Her first signings in June 1967 included Helen Gerstner and Naomi Sims – one of America's first Black supermodels.

As an agent, Wilhelmina saw herself as a mother figure and offered models the kind of advice she wished she had had starting out. She set new working regulations and made having an agent a standard in the industry. But she also shared many controversial views on dieting and beauty and openly acknowledged that she rarely ate to maintain her own proportions.

Wilhelmina had obsessed over fashion magazines since childhood, describing the elegant women that looked back at her from the pages as her glamorous idols. Born Gertrude Behmenburg in Culemborg, Holland, and raised in Oldenburg, Germany, she migrated with her family to Chicago in 1954 when she was 15. After she graduated from high school, she and a friend made the rounds at the city's numerous modelling and etiquette schools, vying for a place. She invented the stage name Winnie Hart.

It wasn't much help – after a great deal of rejection, Winnie took a job as a secretary in a fabric factory. When working at the 1959 International Trade Show in Chicago, she met Shirley Hamilton – the first agent to give her a chance. Assignments with local photographer Kenneth Heilbron followed and helped her to shape her approach. →

> ## " MOST OF ALL I WANT TO SEE THE WORLD, AND MODELLING WILL HELP ME DO IT. "

In 1960 she changed her name to Wilhelmina, went to Europe and arrived with two months of bookings already secured. Her Chicago agents had collaborated with Dorian Leigh's Paris agency to spread the word and high fashion assignments for Dior and Chanel were now hers. Her debut cover was the December 1960 issue od *L'Officiel* – she was photographed in the Sahara Desert wearing a pink Madame Grès hood.

When she returned to New York in 1961, Eileen Ford signed Wilhelmina to a contract. The major covers came in from there – she was in demand, and famous for her work ethic and speed, typically arriving to set in her limousine with her makeup already done.

In a single day, she could reportedly complete seven shoots around Manhattan, banking covers for *McCall's* and the *Ladies' Home Journal*, as well as adverts spanning Battelstein's department store and Pall Mall cigarettes.

Ahead of her 23rd birthday, she reflected on her achievements in an interview with the *Chicago Sun-Times*. 'I worked hard, and I made it. With any luck, I can work nine or 10 more years. Most of all I want to see the world, and modelling will help me do it.'

She kept up this pace until 1964 when she was booked for an appearance on *The Tonight Show*. She met the television producer Bruce Cooper and the following February they were married.

She founded her agency two years later, working with her husband. The Wilhelmina agency still runs today, representing more than 100 models.

VERUSCHKA

VERUSCHKA VON LEHNDORFF
//
14 May 1939

Veruschka's first home was a castle – it was a 40-door journey from her bedroom to the kitchen at the family seat, Steinort, in East Prussia. Born Vera Gottliebe Anna Gräfin von Lehndorff, her mother was a countess, and her father was a leader in the German resistance. He was killed for his part in the 20 July 1944 attempt to assassinate Adolf Hitler.

The rest of the family lost everything but their lives. Aged 5, Vera and her two sisters were detained separately from their pregnant mother. After the war, they were reunited but displaced and she spent the rest of her childhood in flight, attending 13 schools. She was already 6 feet tall by her early teens.

Eventually, the von Lehndorffs arrived in Hamburg and Vera enrolled on a curtain-making course at the city's College of Design. A picture of her taken at art school, eating an apple in the snow, caught the attention of the Italian photographer Ugo Mulas who invited her, in 1959, to shoot a portfolio with him in Florence.

She began trying to find an agent, visiting Dorian Leigh's agency in Paris and Eileen Ford in New York. Both turned her down.

In 1962 she spent almost a year in Italy with the photographer Johnny Moncada. Their experiments resulted in a cache of over 3,000 photos, trialling poses and facial expressions that were not typical of the decade's popular op-art style. →

American *Vogue*, April 1966, photographer Franco Rubartelli.

'The other day I worked with an Italian photographer who allowed me to be myself – even if that meant looking sad or melancholy,' the young Vera wrote to her mother – a conversation later relayed in the 2014 book *From Vera to Veruschka*. 'I cannot tell you how liberating this is.'

She decided to return to New York in 1963, not as Vera, but in character as 'Veruschka'.

Irving Penn immediately took notice of the woman who arrived at his office all in black, her long limbs dressed as if to appear spidery. He called Diana Vreeland, who was now editing American *Vogue*. Veruschka was challenged to produce her portfolio but boldly retorted that Penn and Vreeland ought to impress her with some ideas as to how they would shoot her.

Vreeland was infatuated and from then on championed Veruschka's wild, hypnotic look – a romantic counterpoint to the static debutante or graphic space-age shoots she had otherwise been commissioning at the magazine.

Veruschka shot her first inside editorials for *Vogue* with Penn and posed for Salvador Dalí wearing a whip of shaving foam as a living sculpture. By October 1964 Penn had shot her first *Vogue* cover, wearing an embroidered headscarf and exaggerated winged eyeliner. In 1965 alone, she banked five more.

Increasingly, Veruschka blurred the lines between art and fashion photography. She was actively involved in developing shoot concepts, and brought her own ideas to Vreeland, who almost always said yes. She explored body painting and sculptural hairstyles to challenge beauty ideals.

Given that she saw modelling as a form of acting, it was perhaps inevitable that Veruschka might end up in film. Her opening scene in the cult movie *Blow Up* (1966), with just a single line – 'Here I am!' – secured her global fame. Firmly a supermodel, she made the cover of *LIFE* magazine in August 1967, dubbed 'Bizarre, Exotic, Six Feet Veruschka – The Girl Everybody Stares At'.

In 1971, Diana Vreeland was out at *Vogue* – new editrix Grace Mirabella was in. It was a direct request from Mirabella that prompted Verusckha to move on from fashion modelling and pursue her other artistic interests, less than 10 years after she had started out.

'I was booked for American *Vogue*'s big collections story, and they asked me to cut my hair so I could be more relatable,' she later told *Dazed* magazine. 'I refused to. I knew my moment had passed.'

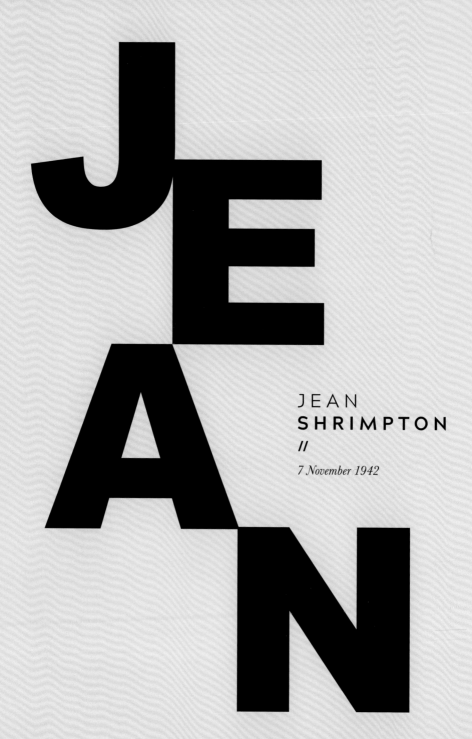

JEAN

JEAN
SHRIMPTON
//
7 November 1942

At the Lucie Clayton Charm Academy in London, models undertook 'grooming and deportment' classes, covering subjects from how to do your own makeup, to flower arranging.

In 1960, a 17-year-old Jean Shrimpton enrolled after scraping a pass at the Langham Secretarial College. Completion of the finishing school's short course allowed her to sign with its associated modelling agency. She registered as Jean Abbatt-Shrimpton, changing her name temporarily to get onto the first page of her new agency's bookings directory.

Using an A–Z map, Jean would travel around London to audition for catalogue jobs. She posed for clients as diverse as the *Daily Express* and the Flour Advisory Board – in one national newspaper campaign she daintily held triangle-cut sandwiches while extolling the virtues of eating white bread.

Jean was working with photographer Brian Duffy, shooting an advert for Kellogg's Corn Flakes, when she first met David Bailey. The almost-aristocratic beauty from Buckinghamshire became a muse to the East End photographer who was shaking up high fashion media with his youthful, sexy images. Three months later, the pair began dating.

Although she had appeared in British *Vogue* editorials before, it was Bailey who captured Jean's first cover for June 1962 – a single, heavily-lined eye and arched eyebrow were the only parts of her visible beneath a large daisy-covered hat. Their romance fuelled the tabloids, and she became famous, nicknamed 'The Shrimp'. Bailey and Jean, with friends like The Rolling Stones, defined London's 'Swinging Sixties' movement. →

The fascination with Jean's off-duty image was pertinent to her success – she was one of the first supermodels to be considered an 'It-girl'. By her own admission, she was authentically 'scruffy', which offered a different aesthetic entirely to the poised models of the 1950s.

'[I was] the real me and not a carbon copy of someone else,' she wrote in her 1964 memoir, titled *The Truth About Modelling*. 'I believe that unless you are prepared to have faith in your own individuality, and your own style, and then project it, you have no chance.'

Jean became a cover girl for *Brides*, *Harper's Bazaar* and *Vanity Fair*. *Glamour* named her Model of the Year. Bailey took her to New York for her first American *Vogue* shoot in February 1962, and she landed on the cover 20 times in total, photographed by Irving Penn, Bert Stern and Richard Avedon. She and Bailey split in 1964.

In her memoir, Jean stated that she could now command an 'immense' £5,000 per year in the United Kingdom and £20,000 in the United States. Her guide to the industry may have been written after just three and a half years of working, but she hoped to offer practical and honest advice

> " [I WAS] THE REAL ME AND NOT A CARBON COPY OF SOMEONE ELSE. "

to the many young women of the era who now wanted to copy her success. The 'secretaries with good measurements and poor shorthand [who] imagine themselves lazing on location in the Bahamas', as she called them.

At the very least, most women wanted to copy her fringe and her mini skirt (she popularized short hems globally, in 1965, when she wore a mini to Australia's Victoria Derby Day).

Jean stopped modelling completely in 1972, at the age of 30. She left London for a life in Cornwall, later opening an antiques shop and running a hotel with her husband Michael Cox, who she married in 1979.

In the rare interviews she has given since, Jean has maintained that she never wanted to be a model and prefers to live a more reclusive lifestyle. 'I never liked being photographed,' she told *The Guardian* in 2011. 'I just happened to be good at it.'

American *Vogue*, December 1970, photographer Arnaud de Rosnay.

LAUREN HUTTON
//
17 November 1943

Mary Laurence Hutton could catch a rattlesnake with her bare hands. As a child born in Charleston, South Carolina, and raised in Tampa, Florida, she spent most of her time in the swamplands, fishing and climbing trees. She didn't learn to read until she was 11.

It was the potent mix of wanderlust and a bad breakup with a boyfriend that led her to New York City to try modelling. She initially worked as a cocktail waitress in Manhattan's Playboy Club and dropped the name Mary to become Lauren Hutton.

When she walked into the Christian Dior store on 7th Avenue, in 1966, and asked for a $62.50-a-week job as a showroom model, she charmed the manager despite having no prior experience.

'I lied through my teeth when they asked if I'd ever modelled,' she told the *Daily News* in 1970. 'When they told me to walk, I mimicked something I'd seen on television.' →

Lauren soon realized that editorial models could make more in an hour than she did in a week as a showroom girl. So, when she met Japanese photographer Carl Shiraishi at a party and he asked if she'd like to try photographic modelling, she said yes. Shiraishi took some test shots and showed them to his friend Eileen Ford, who signed her to her agency. Ford then introduced her to Diana Vreeland at *Vogue*.

For November 1966, Lauren shot the first of her 26 American *Vogue* covers. Bert Stern's image (bouncy hair whipped into a big quiff) was followed in quick succession by another seven before 1968. Lauren's ascent was rapid – you could flick through the magazines at this time to find her shot by Gianni Penati and styled in paisleys in one story and starring in Chanel adverts by Richard Avedon on the next page.

In most of her earliest pictures, Lauren covered up what we would later know to be one of her beauty signatures. It was typically requested that she plug up her gap-tooth smile, so she carried a choice of four teeth covers, alongside her six hairpieces and assorted bras, in her modelling kit bag. At one point, she was even using mortician's wax to hide the 'flaw'.

By 1971 she was firmly *Vogue*'s golden girl – Diana Vreeland relied on her image to sell magazines, her classic beauty proving to bring in reliable sales figures, following the more artsy turn of Veruschka and the ultra-youthful Twiggy.

She signed her history-making deal with Revlon's Ultima cosmetics line in 1963, setting something of a benchmark for all future supermodels to aspire to. At a time when most were paid hourly for their work, she signed an exclusive contract to earn $1 million over three years, committing to 20 days of work a year. It changed her life, and the industry forever – she paved the way for models to be paid like sports stars, with average fees jumping from $300 per day to $1,500 seemingly overnight.

With the feminist movement gaining momentum across America, Lauren's headline-making win made her a poster woman. She embodied the values a whole generation of women aspired to: beautiful, powerful and independently rich.

NAOMI **SIMS**

//

30 March 1948 – 1April 2009

Naomi Sims experienced rejection and racism throughout her career. But her determination to succeed as a supermodel was unwavering, and she unequivocally changed the fashion industry.

She achieved so many firsts in the field – Naomi was the first Black model to be featured on the cover of a national women's magazine in America (*Ladies' Home Journal*) and the first to be given a colour-printed magazine spread in American *Vogue*.

But before all that, what she first wanted was an agent. Naomi had moved from her foster-parents' home in Pittsburgh, Pennsylvania, to New York City in June 1966, with a scholarship to study textiles and management at the Fashion Institute of Technology. She needed money, and her school counsellor suggested modelling on the side.

Donyale Luna had just become the first Black model on the cover of British *Vogue*, giving Naomi hope for change in the United States. But she faced total exclusion from all the agencies she applied to and visited in New York.

Undeterred, she cleverly switched her attention to contacting photographers directly by herself. Gosta Peterson, a house photographer at *The New York Times*, agreed to shoot Naomi and put her, dressed in a black hat and cape, on the cover of the paper's August 1967 supplement *Fashions of The Times*. →

LIFE magazine, October 1969, photographer Yale Joe.

It was a huge statement of confidence in Naomi, who took copies of the magazine to show Wilhelmina Cooper just as she was founding her own agency. Cooper allowed Naomi to circulate 100 issues to advertising agencies – which, unlike fashion magazines, had a mandate for racial representation – with her business card stapled to the cover. Cooper wouldn't go so far as to sign her, yet, but she was willing to endorse her and take a commission on any work that came from the exercise.

Within days, Naomi was on Wilhelmina's books. A call had come in for her to shoot a television commercial for the telecoms giant AT&T, making Naomi the first Black woman to star in a TV network advert. From there came interest from *Vogue* and *Cosmopolitan*, as well as catwalk work for Halston, Bill Blass and Bergdorf Goodman. She started to travel for shoots in December 1968, and by July had been to Hawaii, Argentina, Peru and Greece.

'Maybe I was the right girl at the right time,' she told *The New York Daily News* in 1969. 'I suppose in our times there is a certain point when beauty surpasses prejudice.'

Naomi's landmark *Ladies' Home Journal* cover was released in November 1968. A year on, her portraits made the cover of *LIFE* magazine – the cover line read 'Black models take center stage'. In July 1969, *The New York Times* ran a profile with 'the woman who broke the mold'. Naomi was 21 years old.

When models looked typically moody, and aloofness was the theme of the era, Naomi's selling point was her smile.

'Her special quality is a kind of inner joyousness that breaks through the printed page or television screen,' *The New York Times* described.

In 1972 Naomi married and diversified her career, launching a successful cosmetics and hair-care business that earned more than $5 million within five years. She had been inspired by the thousands of letters she had received as a model, from women asking her for beauty advice.

Portrait taken during the filming of *Twiggy in Hollywood*, 1967, directed by photographer Bert Stern.

TWIGGY

//

19 September 1949

TWIGGY

When The Beatles first landed at New York's John F. Kennedy International Airport in 1964, they were already so famous in America that they were mobbed by fans on arrival. The anticipation was comparable for Twiggy in March 1967 – after just a year of modelling, she too had become a global pop-culture phenomenon.

Twiggy gave a press conference as soon as she got off the plane. She was 17, and she stuck her tongue out for the 50 waiting reporters. She had the face, figure and attitude that embodied London's infectious 'youthquake'. 'The working-class girl with money in her pocket can be as chic as the debutante,' said Cecil Beaton. 'That's what Twiggy is all about.' With her cockney accent and catchy nickname, Lesley Hornby from Neasden energized the fashion world and firmly pushed out the posh and haughty look in modelling.

She was discovered in January 1966 when she had her hair cut short at the high-end salon Leonard of Mayfair. The owner, Leonard Lewis, was looking for someone to trial a new boyish crop on – Twiggy obliged, and afterwards took the bus to photographer Barry Lategan's studio. The resulting pictures were hung in Leonard's salon window, and he showed them to a friend – Deirdre McSharry, fashion editor at the *Daily Express*.

McSharry liked the haircut but loved the model. She arranged a shoot and feature, naming Twiggy 'The Face of 1966'.

Her accompanying copy reads like a prophecy. 'This is the name – Twiggy – because she is branch slim, bends to every shape in fashion and has her hair cut like a cap made of leaves. This is the look that from this moment will launch thousands of clothes … and cause a sell-out in eye pencils.' →

Twiggy's career accelerated faster than perhaps any other model to that date. In less than a month she had completed shoots for *Petticoat*, *Honey*, *Brides*, *Look* and *Fabulous*, then British *Vogue*. She was suddenly a recording artist, with a debut single called 'Beautiful Dreams'.

Her boyfriend of a year, Justin de Villeneuve, had been by her side at every moment of her trajectory, accompanying her on all jobs and taking the role of her manager. It was he who encouraged Twiggy's transformation from model to marketer, to a level that few have managed to replicate. Twiggy Enterprises Limited, directed by Twiggy, Justin, her father and mother, produced merchandise lines spanning dresses and false eyelashes, dolls, board games and lunchboxes.

America was infatuated – on arrival she scored covers for American *Vogue*, *Seventeen*, *Mademoiselle*, *Ladies' Home Journal* and *McCalls*. The New Yorker ran 50 pages on the 'Twiggy Phenomenon'. *Vogue* described her as an 'extravaganza that makes the look of the sixties'. Tours of Japan, Germany and France followed. She released her first autobiography and, in 1969, aged 20, she taped an episode of *This Is Your Life*.

" YOU CAN'T BE A CLOTHES HANGER FOR YOUR ENTIRE LIFE. "

For all the furore, Twiggy faced ample criticism, too. Reporters took issue with her androgynous figure or tried to make her look unintelligent by quizzing her on history, and reporting on how many times she said 'dunno' in an interview.

But for all her naivety and shyness, the teenager was sharp enough to know that fashion was fickle, and that the hype likely wouldn't last.

Twiggy 'retired' in 1970, declaring, 'You can't be a clothes hanger for your entire life.' She planned a music career, and also worked on screen and in the theatre – her role in *The Boy Friend* (1971) won her two Golden Globe awards.

She has modelled rarely since – but the photographs taken in that four-year frenzy are some of the most important and influential of all time.

PAT

PAT
CLEVELAND
//

23 June 1950

Atop a runway made of shaky town hall tables in 1966, Pat Cleveland mastered her walk. It was a walk perhaps better described as a dance – when Pat is on the runway her body is like ribbon, moving almost as one with the fabric she is wearing.

Pat was on tour with *Ebony* magazine's Fashion Fair. Aged 16, she was the youngest model of the 10 on the bus, stopping to put on runway shows at convention centres and churches from New York to Georgia. The experience opened her eyes early on to the travel opportunities that fashion could offer, but also to the racism and division that was deep-rooted, particularly in the southern states, in 1960s America.

Growing up in New York, the daughter of an African American artist and a Swedish jazz saxophonist, Pat had been surrounded by creatives her whole life. She was a designer before she became a model; while still at high school, she made mini skirts and sold them to a local boutique.

She was wearing a houndstooth mini dress of her own design when she was stopped on the subway by Amanda Crider, a fashion assistant at *Vogue*. Crider complimented her look and gave her a business card. →

Buoyed by the experience, Pat asked a friend of her mother's, Addie Passen, to take some portraits, which she then sent out to a handful of New York magazines. She received several rejection letters, but *Ebony's* co-founder Eunice Johnson had replied.

After the *Ebony* tour, Pat signed with the American Girls Agency and worked hard making clothes and modelling simultaneously. She switched to Wilhelmina Cooper's group and had shoots in the debut *Essence* magazine in May 1970.

The same year, Pat was invited to *Vogue's* offices, to show her designs to fashion editor Carrie Donovan. Another editor, Joel Schumacher, crashed the meeting – his model booking for the day hadn't shown up, might Pat fill in? She was whisked off in a limo and photographed by Berry Berenson in Central Park for the magazine's June issue. She was also given the two-page spread as an up-and-coming designer, for which she had originally come in.

Pat got to know more people in the industry, including the designer Halston whom she had met at a party. He asked her to be in his early catwalk shows – she knew exactly how to move in his exquisitely draped clothes.

Despite having been photographed several times for *Vogue* by the likes of Richard Avedon and Irving Penn, by 1971 Pat had still never made the cover. Illustrator Antonio Lopez invited her to Paris, and Pat vowed not to return to work in New York until a Black model had fronted *Vogue*.

In Paris, she lived with Karl Lagerfeld and a coterie of broke, young artist friends. At night, once the illustrators and designers had finished sketching their muses for the day, the set partied at Le Palace nightclub. Fashion was integral to the scene – everyone got dressed up.

By day, Pat started modelling for all the biggest Parisian houses – Christian Dior, Valentino, Yves Saint Laurent and Thierry Mugler, as well as for Lagerfeld who was then at Chloé. In November 1973, she was one of 36 models to take to the stage in the Battle of Versailles, the storied catwalk show that pitted American designers and models against their French counterparts, to raise money to restore the historic palace. In front of an elite audience that spanned celebrities and royalty, Pat's profile soared.

True to her word, Pat returned to New York when Beverly Johnson starred on *Vogue's* cover in 1974. Halston's label was booming with new financial backing, and Pat became his 'Halstonette'.

This was her moment – the public interest in New York's fashion scene peaked and the pair epitomized Studio 54 nightclub glamour. Pat turned catwalking into a performance art – her theatrical approach is legendary to this day. →

Q&A

with

PAT CLEVELAND

What inspired your signature walk? Is there a mood, or feeling, you try to evoke?
Have rhythm in your soul, have your eyes on where you are going and do your best. It's all about building confidence and that starts with how you think from the inside out. That's how I do my best. That's how I do it.

> "
> **HAVE RHYTHM IN YOUR SOUL, HAVE YOUR EYES ON WHERE YOU ARE GOING AND DO YOUR BEST.**
> "

You relocated to Paris in 1971. What did you love about this period of your early career?
Paris was fertile ground to bring in a new energy from the youth of that time. Coming out of the fashion and art world, our entourage was sparkling with hope and full of positive energy. There was Antonio Lopez, Juan Ramos, Karl Lagerfeld, Donna Jordan, Cory Tippin and the new look of designer Stephen Burrows. The Americans had our pop-art ways, and the French loved us for being authentic and showing our talents in the very best way that we could. We dressed to impress and we were superstars, fresh out of the factory of the underground art world and fresh out of school. We had a winning formula, we felt it, and we expressed it. Paris was our challenge, an opportunity to learn and blend into the fabulous culture of art and couture, and the nightlife in Paris was bubbling. Champagne, dancing, beautiful boys in tuxedos, couture shows and cabaret au Paris. Ooh la la!

American *Vogue*, February 1973, photographer Bob Stone.

When you returned to New York, fashion and nightlife were intertwined. What was that moment like?

Halston was all about limo life. One night, my friend Steve Rubel, who had not even opened the door to Studio 54 [to the public], asked if I would bring a friend to the club. I took Halston to Studio 54 for his very first time and he loved it so much that he kept going and bringing along all his friends. It was super glamorous after that – it was beaded dresses, shining bright, disco lights and stars all dancing the night away.

What have you loved most about this job, looking back on decades of glamour?

So much happened on this fashion path I was allowed to be on. Travelling to exotic locations for fashion shoots all over the world with the most famous photographers, working for the best designers. I have enjoyed so many moments.

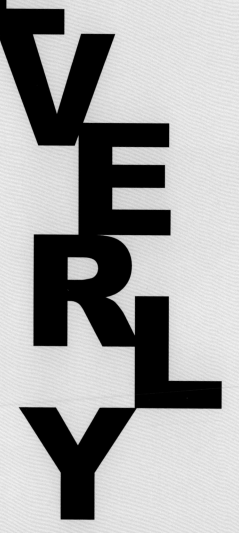

American *Vogue*, March 1974, photographer Bob Stone.

BEVERLY

BEVERLY
JOHNSON
//

13 October 1952

Even as she was putting on her Bulgari diamond earrings, preparing to shoot for American *Vogue* with photographer Francesco Scavullo, Beverly Johnson had no idea that she was making fashion history. It wasn't until the August 1974 issue came out that she was told she was the first Black woman to star on the magazine's cover.

Before that moment, Beverly had been a steady and successful editorial model, with multiple covers for *Glamour* to her name. She had shot with Irving Penn and Richard Avedon for *Vogue*'s inside pages and pattern packets. She was represented by Eileen Ford, had travelled the world, and was recognized in the street.

But for Beverly, who as a teenager had been a competitive swimmer in the Junior Olympics, getting a *Vogue* cover was the equivalent of winning a gold medal.

'I wanted to be at the top of that profession,' she would later recall in American *Vogue*'s video series 'Behind the Moment'.

She grew up in Buffalo, New York, where her mother was a nurse and her father a steelworker. Inspired by the civil rights movement that she had watched unfold on television in the 1960s, she decided she wanted to pursue a degree in Criminal Justice at Northeastern University. →

After high school, she held a part-time job at a local boutique, The Jenny Shop. The manager suggested that if she ever changed her mind about becoming a lawyer, she could try modelling. She gave her a telephone number for a friend at the Manhattan store, Jax, who in turn had a contact at Condé Nast.

Beverly completed her freshman year at university, but when she needed a job on her summer break in June 1971, she remembered she had that card.

Her mother helped her to arrange the appointment with Alexander Lieberman, then editorial director at Condé Nast, and she accompanied her to the Madison Avenue publishing house. Beverly waited all day, but walked out with an assignment; a 10-day trip to Fire Island to shoot with photographer Frank Horvat for *Glamour* magazine.

The editor of *Glamour*, Ruth Whitney, and fashion director Jean Guilder were quick to realize how good Beverly was – they booked her for six *Glamour* covers in two years.

Readers all over America loved her smile. The magazine regularly surveyed its readers: 'Would you like to look like this model?' and 'Would you like to be her friend?' From Dallas to Detroit, the response from readers around the country was the same: they wanted to *be* her.

In 1973, Beverly asked Ford to help take her career to the next level, and listed three goals: she wanted a cosmetics contract, a beauty book deal and a spot on the cover of *Vogue* magazine. When Ford told her it wouldn't be possible, she changed agents and signed with Wilhelmina Cooper.

In less than a year, Beverly posed in a sky-blue Angora knit and diamond earrings for her seminal *Vogue* portraits (seen on p.62).

The impact afterwards may have been unexpected for her, but it was seismic. She went on Larry King's chat show, she was interviewed in *The New York Times* and dubbed 'the super-girl next door'.

A year later, she appeared on commentator Jack O'Brian's radio show. 'You're the biggest Black model in the business,' O'Brian said. 'No, I'm not,' Beverly responded. 'I'm the biggest model – period.'

More *Vogue* covers came her way, as did *Essence*, *Cosmopolitan* and French *Elle*. She crossed over into runway modelling, walking for Halston in New York and Chanel in Paris.

Her success was met with some jealousy from other models, and the *Vogue* editor Grace Mirabella initially wouldn't acknowledge Beverly's achievement in the press. But, as time passed, Beverly got the recognition she deserved; her pictures have left an indelible mark on contemporary culture.

Q&A

with

BEVERLY JOHNSON

What are your memories from your iconic *Vogue* cover shoot? Did it feel like a big deal at the time?

You never know when you do a *Vogue* shoot if you're going to be on page 40 or the cover. My agent called me the morning it hit the newsstands to say, 'Beverly, you just made history.' I raced from my apartment to the newsstand and there were stacks of *Vogue* magazines with my photo on the cover. I stared in utter disbelief until the guy said, 'Ma'am, that'll be fifty cents.' I had raced out without my purse … I didn't know that I was the first. But that moment was life-changing in ways that are hard to describe. My life went into hyperdrive and, truth be told, it hasn't stopped.

What were your first impressions of the fashion and beauty industries when growing up?

I didn't know they existed. I was on the swim team; I was thinking about law school. I thought more about astrophysics than fashion – and trust me, I never thought about astrophysics. Fashion didn't exist in my world. I thought I was ugly. The fashion industry wasn't part of my awareness.

When you first signed with an agency, what was that moment like?

I went to all the agencies including the one Black agency and they all said no. Eileen Ford said no, but later found out that I had done a ten-page spread for *Glamour* magazine, so she changed her mind. What was that moment like? It was like plucking victory from the jaws of defeat. →

American *Vogue*, August 1974, photographer Francesco Scavullo.

" I THOUGHT MORE ABOUT ASTROPHYSICS THAN FASHION – AND TRUST ME, I NEVER THOUGHT ABOUT ASTROPHYSICS. "

Your mother accompanied you to your very first meeting, with *Glamour*. What did her support mean to you?
I didn't take her; she took me. My dad was against it because being a model and being a streetwalker were different terms for the same profession in his mind. We sat in the lobby – they thought I was there to take a typing test. People would come out, look at me and go behind closed doors. I guess they decided I'd be okay for a *Glamour* magazine shoot. It just ignited. In hindsight my mother was supportive, but the whole venture seemed like a whim.'

Of your earliest jobs, what are some of your favourite memories?
So, you don't want to hear about all the guys who offer you the world but want just one thing? You said favourite memories, sorry. My third job was the first Black fashion magazine, *Essence*. I was on the ground floor of something we never thought we'd see. A Black fashion magazine was like a green Martian magazine. It was absolutely groundbreaking, and I was there as it launched.

JANICE
DICKINSON
//

16 February 1955

Getting out of Florida was Janice Dickinson's number one priority as a teenager. She would spend hours reading fashion magazines in the aisles of her local supermarket rather than going home after school, to escape a hostile and abusive family environment.

Lauren Hutton was her idol, and she joined the John Powers Modelling School in the hope of pursuing a career that looked something like hers. When an opportunity to compete in a national modelling contest came up, Janice was determined to succeed. She copied an outfit that model Karen Graham was wearing on the cover of *Vogue* – a silk turban and V-neck dress – and was crowned 'Miss High Fashion Model' of 1972, beating hundreds of other hopefuls.

Wilhelmina Cooper signed Janice, but as blonde models ruled the scene in New York, she faced a lot of rejection and struggled to build her portfolio. As she was of Polish and Irish descent, with dark hair, Cooper thought that she might find more work in Europe and sent her to Paris via the French agency Christa Models.

Janice's career was made in Paris. In 1975 she was photographed for seven French *Elle* covers in a row (at that time the magazine came out weekly). Duffy captured her in a bandana, and Alice Springs in a soaked white shirt. On the inside pages, she wore Chanel tweeds with a sultry pout as the star of the brand's cosmetics campaigns. →

c.1979, photographer Horst P. Horst.

Janice was a rebel supermodel in the sense that she was unapologetically herself, rather than presenting a quaint or wholesome version of her image that some designers might prefer. She worked with Azzedine Alaïa and Gianni Versace – artists who dressed her in armour and amplified her personality. Her look appealed to photographers like Guy Bourdin who shot moody portraits of her for French *Vogue*.

In Paris and Milan, Janice caused a stir – her outspoken nature often got her into trouble, and she partied as hard as she worked. But by the time she returned to New York in 1977, she had shot with most of Europe's best designers and photographers.

After a brief time with Ford, she signed with Elite Model Management, which was newly opening in America and looking for models to propel as celebrity personalities. She seamlessly joined the Studio 54 social set, and her relationships with famous actors of the day fuelled tabloid interest.

Firmly a supermodel by now, her work escalated further to include lucrative commercials with Coca-Cola and JVC cameras. Her high fashion assignments continued alongside – she remained a catwalk regular, walking for designers Perry Ellis and Oscar de la Renta, as well as shooting adverts for Versace and Calvin Klein and countless *Cosmopolitan* covers.

Janice ultimately began to diversify her career into television hosting, and eventually reality television programming. She harnessed the power of her celebrity and could see value in the fashion industry as a source of entertainment. Her two tell-all memoirs are packed with controversial stories – a truly unfiltered version of events. →

Q&A

with

JANICE DICKINSON

What qualities did you have, when starting out, that helped you succeed as a model?
When I first went to New York I saw how competitive the women were. I was still in high school, but I knew how to compete – I was on the baseball team and the swim team. I knew you had to have a certain kind of composure and attitude. Plus, a bit of snobbism. I didn't feel beautiful before I started modelling; I felt okay. But suddenly you have people pampering you – hair, makeup, stylists. They're saying, 'Beautiful, gorgeous, divine!' I didn't feel that I had all these traits people were telling me I had, but I started to believe it.

"

THEY'RE SAYING, 'BEAUTIFUL, GORGEOUS, DIVINE!' I DIDN'T FEEL THAT I HAD ALL THESE TRAITS PEOPLE WERE TELLING ME I HAD, BUT I STARTED TO BELIEVE IT.

"

American *Vogue*, May 1977, photographer Francesco Scavullo.

You then went to Paris to work on your portfolio ...

Back in those days, there were no computers, no cell phones. You had a portfolio of pictures and carried it to every appointment. My book wasn't very good when I arrived in Paris, so I had to work to round it out. You needed a mix of high fashion and commercial pictures, natural, outdoorsy shots, girl in suit, girl sitting in a bar, bathing-suit pictures taken in the South of France ... You needed that range. Mine ended up as thick as a phone book.

Which photographers championed you early on?

Helmut Newton flew me to St Tropez and wanted to shoot nudes for a book cover. I didn't want to do that job, but I met his wife, June Newton, who took photographs under the pseudonym Alice Springs. She said, 'He might not want to shoot you again, but I will.' She shot for French *Elle* – she could pick up the phone and tell them, 'I've just met this girl, Janice Dickinson, and I think she'd be right for the cover.' And that's exactly what happened.

You became known as an industry rebel. Did this ever backfire?

I made some solid friends in the fashion industry, but I also made a lot of enemies. When I first got to Italy, I met Gianni Versace. I told him that his clothes were divine and that I hoped he would book me. My next appointment was over at Giorgio Armani's, but I called him Gianni by mistake. He thought I was making fun of him and told me to get out. I was crying and went back to Gianni, who was thrilled. He loved the story so much that he made me his top model for years after. He loved that I was cheeky. I wasn't always trying to stir the pot. Sometimes, it was these accidental things that shot me to the top.

What was it like when you returned to America as a supermodel?

I took New York by storm. I turned down all the photographers that were mean to me in the beginning. It was very exciting. I think I was the first model who was the biggest print model, but who also had a full share of runway shows. It used to be one or the other, but for me, it became a total hodgepodge of working across television, print, high fashion, commercials. I worked night and day, from 6am to 7pm, and then 7pm to 1am. And then I found time to go to Studio 54. Honey, there was always time to party.

LMAN

IMAN
//
25 July 1955

In 1972 Iman Mohamed Abdulmajid became a refugee. Her family fled Mogadishu overnight, crossing the Somalian border into Kenya to seek asylum.

At home, she had enjoyed a privileged upbringing. Her father was the ambassador to Saudi Arabia, which meant travel opportunities, ambassadorial residences and chauffeurs, as well as a stellar education. However, the aftermath of the 1969 military coup brought instability, and her family was forced to leave. 'All of a sudden, you're a refugee with nothing,' she recalled, in an interview with British *Vogue* in 2022.

Iman has credited the NGO workers who helped her at this time for inspiring her lifelong commitment to philanthropic work. She found a hostel, then an apartment to live in, a place to study political science at the University of Nairobi, and a part-time job as a hotel waitress – she spoke five languages and was also an asset to the tourism board as a translator.

In 1975 she was approached in the street by the photographer Peter Beard. When Beard asked her how much he could pay, to convince her to pose for an exhibition he was working on, she did the sums. Iman asked for $8,000 – the remaining cost of her tuition. She took a girlfriend with her to the shoot and channelled the performance of Umm Kulthum, one of her favourite actresses. The resulting portraits (done without a hair and makeup team) showed a natural beauty, but the events also revealed a savvy businesswoman.

Six months later Beard got back in touch, this time with support from Wilhelmina Cooper, to whom he had shown Iman's pictures. The pair invited her to New York, on the promise that they could make her a supermodel.

'I had never seen a magazine or worn high heels,' Iman told website Net-a-Porter in 2023. 'But I went, under the caveat they would book me a two-way ticket so that I could leave and not be stuck in America.' →

American *Vogue*, December 1977, photographer Eisuke Ishimuro.

When Iman arrived in Manhattan on 15 October 1975, there was a press welcome party in her honour. One of her first bookings was with Arthur Elgort for American *Vogue*, who captured the newcomer wearing a flash of purple eyeshadow. New York's up-and-coming designers – Bill Blass, Diane von Furstenberg, Calvin Klein and Oscar de la Renta – all hired her to walk in their catwalk shows. She became a fixture at Studio 54 and landed a cosmetics campaign with Revlon.

Iman noticed immediately that often Black models and white models were not being paid the same. She took a stand, told her agent Wilhelmina Cooper that change was needed, and refused work that wasn't equally paid.

Within a few years, she was as successful in Paris as she was in New York and had become a muse to both Azzedine Alaïa and Yves Saint Laurent. The latter dedicated an entire couture collection, 1979's 'The African Queen', to Iman. Appropriately, it was she who modelled the collection for the advertising campaign, shot by photographer David Bailey.

Just four years into her career, Iman also began to diversify her work. She starred in the 1979 film *The Human Factor*, the first in a string of acting roles. The seed for her beauty business, Iman Cosmetics, had apparently been planted at that first shoot with Elgort, when the makeup artist on duty asked if she had brought her own foundation with her.

It wasn't until October 1989, though, that Helmut Newton photographed Iman's 'farewell' shoot announcing her retirement from modelling. Over the years, she has continued to pose for occasional portraits, sometimes with husband David Bowie, to whom she was married from 1992 until his death in 2016.

With friends Bethann Hardison and Naomi Campbell, she formally launched The Diversity Coalition in 2013, spurred by a *New York Times* article which stated that bookings for Black catwalk models were falling. Iman's impact and involvement in the fashion industry are ongoing.

c.1978.

JERRY

JERRY **HALL**

//

2 July 1956

A car crash changed everything for Jerry Hall, in 1972. Recovering at the hospital, she was injected with penicillin but had an allergic reaction – her insurance company paid out $800.

Jerry used the money to buy her ticket out of Mesquite, Texas, where she and her twin sister Terry had grown up the youngest of five girls. She had first shown an interest in modelling at 14, pursuing local agent Kim Dawson and posing in the windows of the boutique, Funky.

By 16, modelling in Europe was a firm ambition. She was desperate to leave home and has frequently described her father as violent, possibly owing to post-traumatic stress disorder after serving in World War II.

Jerry had never been on an aeroplane but bought herself a ticket to Paris. From there she visited St Tropez. The agent Claude Haddad spotted her as she arrived on the beach in a pink metallic bikini and heels. Much to her surprise, her plan to attract attention had worked.

Jerry signed with Haddad, and he set her up in an apartment-share back in Paris with singer Grace Jones, who was then also an up-and-coming model. Assignment number one was with Helmut Newton, who dressed her up in leather, whips and chains, and proclaimed her debut photographs to be art. On the catwalk, it was Yves Saint Laurent who first booked her, putting her in one of his newly famous tuxedos. →

Jerry's peacockish personal style attracted equally creative friends. She met the illustrator Antonio Lopez while wearing a gold suit, with feathers pasted to her forehead. When she hit Club Sept, the Parisian nightlife haunt, she did so in turquoise chiffon and tiger-print dresses – all designer copies made by her mother, until Jerry began earning enough money to buy the real versions.

'I'd never had money before; we were a rather poor family,' she recalled in an interview with *Women's Wear Daily* in 1985. 'By the time I left Paris, I had a full-length Revillon mink cape trimmed with silver fox, designed by Fernando Sanchez. One time, I went into a store and bought every single colour [of] nail polish they had.'

1975 was a defining year for Jerry. She signed with Eileen Ford and moved to New York, seamlessly swapping her Parisian social set for Studio 54. She was painted blue and photographed on the Welsh coast for the cover of Roxy Music's new album *Siren* – her long red hair flowed like lava over the volcanic rock stacks. She started dating the band's frontman, Bryan Ferry, but would become even more famous two years later when she left him for Mick Jagger of The Rolling Stones.

Norman Parkinson also took some of Jerry's most revered pictures for British *Vogue* just three years into her career, in 1975: she wore a red latex swimming cap to dive off a USSR plinth, and tucked a glossy telephone to her ear inside a blue cap for her debut cover. Her editorial success was peaking – she scored covers for *Cosmopolitan*, *Vogue Italia* and *L'Officiel*.

When Yves Saint Laurent debuted his new perfume, Opium, in 1977, he asked Jerry to star in the campaign. She was reunited with Helmut Newton to shoot the provocative advertising campaign; it was so successful it helped sell $30 million worth of the perfume in Europe in its first year alone.

Jerry's super selling power was confirmed, and contracts spanning Revlon cosmetics, Olympus Cameras and Dr Pepper all came her way. Her continued fashion success opened the door to more opportunities, and she later pursued both film and musical theatre roles, on Broadway and in London's West End.

She never stopped modelling, though, on occasion posing with her model daughters, Lizzy and Georgia May Jagger, who both followed in her footsteps.

INÈS
DE LA FRESSANGE
//
11 August 1957

It is impossible to talk about the concept of 'French chic' without mentioning Inès de La Fressange. When she rose to fame in the early 1980s, Karl Lagerfeld decided that she was emblematic of the ideal, and that her looks somewhat resembled the late designer Gabrielle 'Coco' Chanel. He offered her a career-making deal as an exclusive model and ambassador for the brand – which was, back then, a tired couture house that he had just taken the reins of.

Inès was born into a French aristocratic family. Her father was a marquis and a stockbroker, her mother was an Argentine Colombian model. Home was an 18th-century mill on the outskirts of Paris – there was also a townhouse and a Swiss chalet. Her father had his own plane; her grandmother wore couture and drove a gold Rolls Royce. After studying art history at L'École du Louvre, Inès decided to try modelling. She was 18, and one of her first editorial photoshoots was for French *Elle* with photographer Oliviero Toscani. She found catwalk modelling harder to break into, though.

'I had no luck when I started out as a model,' she told *Interview* magazine in 2008. 'It's the only career in the world that you can't choose for yourself – you have to be chosen.'

Connected by a boyfriend who was a musician and a model himself, she signed with the agency Pauline. 'It was the first agency that took girls who were a little offbeat, not just blonde California surfer-types,' she said. →

Paris Match, November 1983, photographer Jean-Claude Sauer.

" IT'S THE ONLY CAREER IN THE WORLD THAT YOU CAN'T CHOOSE FOR YOURSELF – YOU HAVE TO BE CHOSEN. "

When Inès had initially approached Chanel and Dior, neither of the quintessential French houses had been interested. It was Kenzō Takada, the Japanese designer working in Paris, who was the first to hire her for his catwalk show in 1976.

Following Kenzō's approval, Inès began booking more shows – Sonia Rykiel, Dior, Lanvin, Jean Paul Gaultier and, occasionally, Chanel. She became known as the 'talking mannequin', for the way that she so freely sashayed down the runway chatting to the photographers who, in those days, lined the front row rather than standing at the end of the platform.

It was after she walked in Karl Lagerfeld's autumn 1983 Chloé show that she began to spend time with the designer. When he was appointed at Chanel, he was charged with revitalizing the house – Gabrielle Chanel herself had died almost a decade earlier.

25-year-old Inès became his muse, and the first model to sign a contract covering advertising and appearances, as well as catwalk shows. Her likeness to the founder was played upon endlessly – she posed in the late designer's office and starred as Coco in the 1984 Coco perfume campaign, lensed by Paolo Roversi.

'I would not do it without Inès de La Fressange,' Lagerfeld told American *Vogue* in 1986. 'I ask her everything. She tells me what she wants to wear, and I design it.'

Inès's influence on French fashion in the 1980s was now understood around the world. The French Government recognized this and invited her to be the latest celebrity to represent Marianne, the symbol of the French Republic (Catherine Deneuve and Brigitte Bardot had previously held the honour). Accepting the job, however, caused Inès and Lagerfeld to famously fall out – her contract with Chanel was terminated in 1989.

Eventually, the pair became friends again. But even when Inès's career as a Chanel supermodel was over, she was able to sell her vision of French style, globally. She went on to work as a designer and author – her Parisian style guidebooks have sold over a million copies to date.

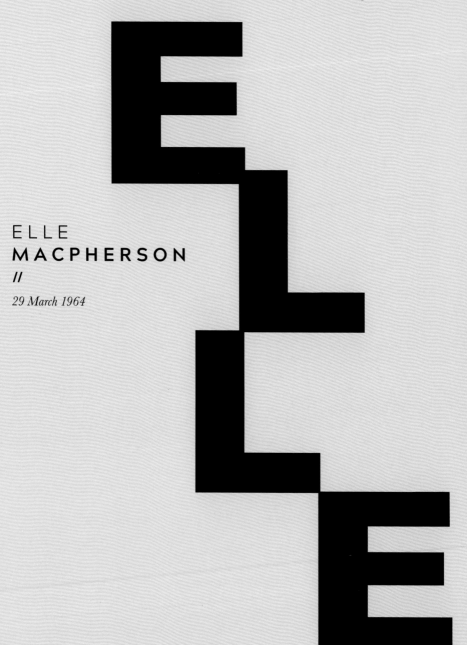

Calvin Klein Jeans, Autumn/Winter 1984.

ELLE
MACPHERSON
//

29 March 1964

Elle Macpherson had only intended to model during her gap year. The plan was to travel to New York City and earn some money, before coming home to study law at the University of Sydney, Australia. She ended up working in America for over 20 years.

Elle's first 'modelling job' had been while still in primary school, when she and another girl from her class posed on the monkey bars for a local newspaper in Killara. But when she shot up to be 6 feet tall as a teenager, she was signed with the Sydney agency Chadwick and began modelling, alongside working in a pharmacy. At home, her biggest hit was a 1982 television commercial for Tab Cola – in a red bikini, she turns heads on the beach while clutching a hot-pink soda can.

On arrival in Manhattan, she took a meeting with Click Model Management – New York agencies were readily recruiting a new wave of beachy blondes from Australia at the time. Elle was signed internationally and moved into an apartment share with Czech model Paulina Porizkova.

Bikini models had rarely been considered for high fashion assignments before. These were separate industries, with their own star talents that appealed to different audiences. But when Elle arrived in America, it was immediately clear that she – with her golden tan and surf-honed physique – would usher in a new athletic body ideal in fashion. →

From the get-go, Elle became an editorial favourite. She knew how to lead a picture with her body, rather than a haughty face, creating fresh, dynamic images. Between 1983 and 1985 she starred in shoots for the Australian, French and American editions of *Cosmopolitan* and *Vogue*, shot by Steven Meisel, Roxanne Lowit and Albert Watson. But it was her work for French *Elle* that came to be defining. One of her first appearances was in the summer of 1983, shot by Hans Feurer and disguised somewhat with dark hair.

When, in 1985, the magazine's creative director and lead photographer Gilles Bensimon began working on the launch issues of American *Elle*, the namesake model became his muse and collaborator. Elle, the supermodel, became almost synonymous with the magazine, featuring in its pages very frequently.

Aged 21, Elle married Bensimon – she wore a custom clinging wedding dress by her friend, the then-rising star designer Azzedine Alaïa. Bensimon photographed her statuesque next to the 5-feet-3-inch Alaïa in what would become an exhibit-worthy image.

Elle was one of the first models who achieved mass audience appeal with titles aimed at men as well as women, adding a new roster of assignments to any future supermodels' checklist.

In 1986, in Bora Bora, she shot her first cover for *Sports Illustrated*'s annual swimsuit issue. The issue sold 1.2 million copies – up from 790,000 the year before. She was booked for three years in a row.

Four years into her career, Elle had achieved a great deal in the editorial sphere but had not yet conquered the catwalk. This changed in March 1986 with a show for Perry Ellis, and Elle began appearing regularly for New York's leading names – Ralph Lauren and Donna Karan.

She quickly reached the pinnacle of the high fashion and couture catwalks in Europe, walking for Azzedine Alaïa, Chanel and Versace – designers who dressed 'The Body', as she became known, in clothes that emphasized her figure.

No matter how many couture bookings Elle was now getting, though, she never saw herself as a 'fashion girl'. She had a head for business and enjoyed commercial jobs. When *TIME* magazine formalized her nickname, Elle saw a personal branding opportunity. Calendars, workout videos and a lingerie and wellness empire would be launched, in succession. The supermodel had turned super mogul.

LINDA
EVANGELISTA
//

10 May 1965

Linda Evangelista didn't win the Miss Teen Niagara beauty pageant in 1981. But what was seemingly a setback for the 16-year-old from St Catharines, Ontario, ended up being fortuitous – she was spotted by a scout from Elite who was in the audience.

Her parents made her wait a few years before formally signing with the agency in 1984. But Linda had always been fashion-obsessed – as a teenager her bedroom walls were covered with tear-outs from *Vogue*.

Despite growing up in a strict Italian Catholic household, Linda had persuaded her mother to let her go to modelling school at the age of 13. At 16, she had been offered the chance to work in Japan. When she was unexpectedly asked to pose for nude photos on arrival, she flew straight home and almost gave up on her dream.

Her agents asked her to give modelling one more chance and to enter the pageant that ultimately led to her breakthrough. Once signed with Elite, she went to Paris and had some immediate success – a cover of *L'Officiel*, and catwalk shows for Karl Lagerfeld at Chanel. →

Linda quickly became known as a good model, but it was a haircut in 1988 that made her a supermodel. Photographer Peter Lindbergh suggested that she should try a more androgynous look. The hairstylist Julien d'Ys was enlisted to cut a short gamine crop. Lindbergh captured a series of photos as it happened – Linda covers her eyes as her ponytail is lopped off in one swoop of the scissors.

A week later, at Milan Fashion Week, Linda had been booked to walk in 20 shows, but 16 designers immediately cancelled her because of the dramatic change to her look. With her time newly freed up, *Vogue Italia* editor Franca Sozzani instead sent her on Concorde back to New York to shoot her debut *Vogue* cover with Steven Meisel.

Linda's career accelerated rapidly – her day-rate quadrupled thanks to the attention her hair had brought, and she had starred on the covers of almost all international editions of *Vogue* by the end of the year. Copycats all over the world now took her pictures to their hairdressers, asking for 'The Linda'. She became known as modelling's greatest chameleon and dyed her crop peroxide blonde and tomato red, depending on what look she fancied that month – crucially, her bookings never faltered because of her hairstyle again.

Along with her contemporaries Christy Turlington, Cindy Crawford, Naomi Campbell and Tatjana Patitz, Linda posed for Lindbergh's seminal British *Vogue* cover portrait in January 1990. *Vogue*'s editor Liz Tilberis had asked Lindbergh to photograph the new woman of the decade – Lindbergh's response was not one woman, but a quintet of beauties who looked strong in their Giorgio di Sant'Angelo bodysuits and Levi's jeans and felt completely fresh when compared to the excess of the 1980s.

George Michael felt inspired and recruited Linda and the new supermodels to lip-sync through his 'Freedom! '90' music video. Gianni Versace, in turn, asked them to repeat the feat on the catwalk.

Linda was already omnipresent in pop culture. Then, in American *Vogue*'s October 1990 issue, she gave in passing what would become the most famous quote in super modelling history.

'We have this expression, Christy and I,' she said. 'We don't wake up for less than $10,000 a day.'

With this comment, often referred to as the 'Let them eat cake!' of the 20th century, Linda had successfully defined the era of the powerful and empowered model – the beauty with a fiery personality, who could command her own fees, work with anyone she wanted and style herself however she wished.

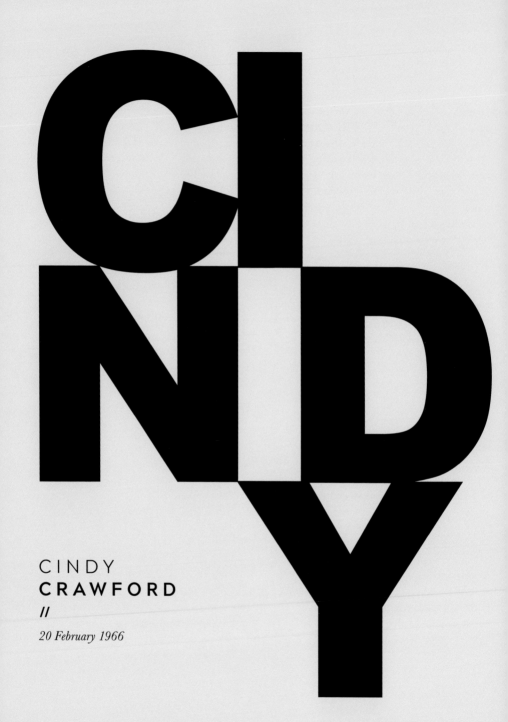

CINDY

CINDY CRAWFORD

//

20 February 1966

Many of Cynthia Crawford's teenage summers were spent detasseling corn, working full days in the fields surrounding her Illinois hometown of DeKalb.

A more glamorous opportunity came up in September 1981, when she was 15. A new local clothing boutique called Bret's asked a group of high-school girls to form a 'fashion board' – we might call them influencers now. In exchange for taking part in an in-store catwalk show and posing for local newspaper *The Daily Chronicle*, the girls were offered a 20 per cent shopping discount.

Of the 15 students selected, Cindy (as Cynthia became known) stood out to the newspaper photographer Roger Legel. As well as covering local stories – from fires to football games – Legel shot a regular 'Coed of the Week' slot for the *DeKalb Nite Weekly* college newspaper. He photographed Cindy by the swimming pool at her then-boyfriend's parents' house and, in November 1982, she appeared on her first editorial cover.

While she had originally planned to be a nuclear physicist, Cindy had already expressed an interest in modelling. On a previous occasion, two classmates had pranked her, telling her to show up at another local store for a modelling job that didn't exist. Her father, a glazier, and mother, who worked in a bank, were, perhaps rightly, suspicious of the industry and told her to focus on her studies.

Legel encouraged Cindy to look for an agent in Chicago, though, and she was signed by Marie Anderson at Stewart Talent. She began doing catalogue shoots, landing her first paid job in 1983 in an advert for department store Marshall Fields. She wore a Cross-Your-Heart bra, and earned $150 for the job, which 'beat working in the cornfields' she would later say in her 2015 memoir *Becoming*. The campaign's photographer James Vaughan later recalled on his Pleasure Photo blog that the brunette he had booked hadn't arrived, so Anderson had talked him into hiring 'this newcomer called Cindy Crawford' instead. →

In October 1983, 17-year-old Cindy told *The Daily Chronicle* that modelling was 'a good way to make money, it's interesting and fun, but I couldn't do it as a career'. Just one month later, though, she entered Elite's debut Look of the Year modelling contest and made the national finals. It was also around this time that she was first pictured by two of Chicago's best-known photographers, Victor Skrebneski and Bob Frame.

Cindy graduated from DeKalb High School in 1984 as the valedictorian of her class. In the autumn, she would be studying chemical engineering at Northwestern University on a full academic scholarship.

But Elite sent her to Paris for the summer to develop her portfolio, and she found that her doe eyes and glossy brunette hair appealed in Europe. Her likeness to Gia Carangi, a favourite model of leading fashion photographers of the time, earned her the nickname 'Baby Gia'. She worked on editorials with Patrick Demarchelier for *Vogue Italia*'s September issue, and the October cover of *20Ans*, by Steve Landis.

Cindy still took up her place at Northwestern but, by the turn of 1985, her career had taken off and she dropped out to pursue modelling full time.

She moved to New York and, in the summer of 1986, she shot her first American *Vogue* cover with Richard Avedon. She would later express her amazement that the mole on her upper lip, which her sisters had teased her about since a child and which so many photographers had previously retouched away, had not been removed. Cindy's beauty mark became a trademark – her 'famous flaw'.

From there, Cindy's bookings spanned the aspirational – from Versace to Chanel – to the accessible – GAP, Revlon and Pepsi. She joined her friends Naomi Campbell, Linda Evangelista, Christy Turlington, and Tatjana Patitz for the landmark January 1990 British *Vogue* cover, which was shot by Peter Lindbergh, and in George Michael's 'Freedom! '90' music video.

She has shot more than 600 magazine covers, diversifying her career beyond modelling into television presenting and entrepreneurship, co-founding Meaningful Beauty in 2004. Her two children, Presley and Kaia Gerber, have also pursued modelling.

TATJANA

TATJANA
PATITZ

//

25 March 1966 – 11 January 2023

In picturesque Skanör, a 7-year-old Tatjana Patitz was obsessed with nothing but horses and white sandy beaches. Her German father (a travel journalist), Estonian mother (a former dancer), she and her sister had moved to the Swedish seaside town from Hamburg, and it was here that Tatjana first fell in love with the natural world.

In November 1983, aged 17, Tatjana walked into a department store in Stockholm where the model agency Elite was sponsoring a national search for new faces. It was the inaugural Look of the Year contest and, with no social media or digital photography, the entire competition was based on Polaroids. The judges placed Tatjana third amongst the entrants from Sweden. Two other future supermodels – Stephanie Seymour and Cindy Crawford – had also entered the international rounds this year, but 15-year-old American Lisa Hollenbeck was crowned the global winner.

Nonetheless, for being a runner-up Tatjana won a trip to Paris and a six-month trial contract with an agent. She found little work until she met Azzedine Alaïa. He booked her to walk in his winter 1985 catwalk show, alongside fellow newcomer Yasmin Le Bon and Alaïa regular Janice Dickinson.

The backing from Alaïa gave Tatjana's editorial bookings a boost. For the August 1985 issue of French *Vogue*, Peter Lindbergh shot her walking through the city's streets with a pram, and smoking cigarettes at the literary haunt Café de Flore. In quick succession, her first British *Vogue* cover was lensed by Albert Watson for the October issue, the brand's logo in piercing blue to match her bright eyes. In the magazine's December edition, she starred in one of Irving Penn's celebrated, eccentric photographs, 'Contact Lenses', with mismatched blue and green lenses. →

American *Vogue*, October 1989, photographer Arthur Elgort.

As Tatjana's profile grew, she was offered bigger commercial campaigns. She moved to New York in 1986 and Bruce Weber photographed her in adverts for Calvin Klein sportswear, known back then as Calvin Klein Classifications. Richard Avedon shot her for his 'Unforgettable Women' series of Revlon commercials in 1987, next to Iman, Jerry Hall and Talisa Soto.

Her debut American *Vogue* cover came out in May 1987, shot by Avedon. In another editorial, with Patrick Demarchelier, the magazine called her 'Tatjana: Million Dollar Beauty'. The corresponding feature posed the question: 'What turns a tomboy into the year's golden girl?'

Tatjana told the magazine that she had made $2 million in 1987, and on one particular assignment had earned $30,000 in a single day. 'Her features are a bit off,' photographer Herb Ritts deemed, for a comment box on the side of the story. 'She's not a typical commercial beauty. But when I shoot her, I'm never bored. Her looks have power, strength and intensity.'

At exactly the time Tatjana's career was reaching new heights, she decided it was time to slow her pace, eschewing the lifestyle many of her peers were enjoying while they lived and partied in New York and Paris. In 1989, the same summer she scored two consecutive American *Vogue* covers, she decided to relocate to California, buying a ranch in Malibu.

Tatjana's supermodel status was sealed in 1990 when she appeared in Peter Lindbergh's iconic January *Vogue* cover lineup, and in George Michael's 'Freedom! '90' music video. She joined Christy Turlington, Naomi Campbell, Linda Evangelista and Cindy Crawford, starring as Michael's undone beauties, prowling around an abandoned London townhouse.

Tatjana resisted fame, though, particularly at the level achieved by the other 'supers' of her era. Surrounded at home by the horses and dogs she loved, she would continue to model and then retreat on her own terms.

'She was far less visible than her peers,' Anna Wintour, editor-in-chief of *Vogue*, recalled in 2023. 'More mysterious, more grown-up, more unattainable – and that had its own appeal.'

CARLA **BRUNI**

//

23 December 1967

An 18-year-old Carla Bruni craved independence. She was also a little bored of travelling some 37 stops on the Métro each week to make it to her architecture classes at the University of Paris. So, when her brother's then-girlfriend, a model, suggested Carla could do it too, she found herself an agent at City Models.

'It was not making money; it was making my *own* money,' she would later tell *Vanity Fair* of her motivations. 'Modelling meant I did not have to rely on my parents or a man. What I wanted was to be free.'

Born in Turin, Carla had spent her early years under the gilded ceilings of the hilltop Piedmontese castle, Castello di Castagneto Po. She was raised the daughter of concert pianist Marisa Borini and the composer and capitalist Alberto Bruni Tedeschi – although she would find out later in life that her biological father was Maurizio Remmert, a classical guitarist. Her legal grandfather was Virginio Bruni Tedeschi, who built his family's fortune in the 1920s when he founded the tyre-manufacturing company CEAT.

Carla's childhood was charmed – opera legend Maria Callas might come over for dinner and a singalong. Carla was encouraged to learn violin and piano, but she was more attracted to the cool than the classical – the first record she bought was David Bowie's *Changes*.

In the mid 1970s, though, the families of Italy's rich industrialists became targets, vulnerable to kidnappings by the Red Brigades terrorist organization. Aged 7, Carla was relocated to France for her safety, then sent to a Swiss finishing school. →

Returning to Paris for university, and studying art and architecture, was a path of which her parents had approved. Her siblings pursued creative careers too – her sister Valeria Bruni Tedeschi became an actress. When Carla dropped out of university in 1986 to try modelling, her parents were protective – her mother acted as her manager, initially.

Carla's earliest catwalk looks spanned the playful Parisian designs of Jean-Charles de Castelbajac and the muted Italian styles of Romeo Gigli. She moved to New York for almost three years, sharing a loft in Tribeca with the actress Marine Delterme and walking for Calvin Klein. Her clique included models Karen Mulder and Farida Khelfa, and she also got to know the supermodels who would become her friends for life, Naomi Campbell and Linda Evangelista.

Signing with the Marilyn agency's Véronique Rampazzo, and moving back to Paris in 1989, led to Carla's own breakthrough as a supermodel. She began working with Chanel – Karl Lagerfeld described her as regal, and 'beyond polite. So many ... had periods of being moody and difficult. She was always perfect.'

In advertising, she was one of the first to be hired by the new American denim brand Guess Jeans. The pictures from her debut advertising assignment, aged 19, became a newsworthy talking point. 'It was scandalous, because I was sitting on the knee of this old man,' she would later say.

Her editorial appearances, particularly in Europe, began to mount up. Carla's debut *Vogue* cover was for the Spanish edition, shot by Randolph Graff; British and Italian issues followed.

The catwalk was her arena, though – she could famously make even the most outré runway outfits look not just plausible, but classy.

She could play Gianni Versace's sexy, high-octane muse as easily as Yves Saint Laurent's chic swan (literally – she would eventually model the designer's 'swan dress'). Fluent in French and Italian fashion moods, she could pull off an ambiguous European elegance like few others.

Perhaps unsurprisingly, given her roots in music, Carla quit modelling at her peak, in 1996, to pursue a fresh career as a recording artist. She was successful in this and the other reinventions she has lived since, from supermodel to chart-topping singer, to, eventually, the 'first lady' of France through her marriage to Nicolas Sarkozy.

STEPHANIE
SEYMOUR

//

23 July 1968

Stephanie Seymour was eating a burger at a downtown café in San Diego when she was 're-discovered'. A rookie agent approached her table to ask if she had ever thought about modelling. She told him she was a university student with classwork to concentrate on. Then she laughed and he realized his mistake – the year was 1988 and the 19-year-old was already one of the most sought-after models in America.

Stephanie had moved back to San Diego at the end of 1987, after three years of living in New York. Shortly after, she would appear on her debut American *Vogue* and *Sports Illustrated* covers becoming, indisputably, a supermodel.

'I think every little girl wants to be a model, or a princess; an Avon Lady, or a movie star,' Seymour told the *Los Angeles Times* in 1988 of her start. 'I was no different.'

Stephanie was 15 when she became a finalist in Elite's Look of the Year competition, joining Cindy Crawford and Tatjana Patitz in the pool of hopefuls that year. Having paid the nominal entry fee, and sent in two photographs her mother had taken, she went through the regional rounds and, finally, to Acapulco, Mexico, where she made the top 10. When she returned home, she did some local work for titles such as *San Diego Home/Garden* magazine, then was signed officially by Elite in 1984. →

American *Vogue*, June 1987, photographer Arthur Elgort.

During her first summer as a professional model, she went to Europe. She posed for French *Vogue* and Italian *Harper's Bazaar* and celebrated her sweet 16 with a birthday party in Rome. At the end of the holidays, her parents allowed her not to return to high school and instead to take correspondence courses and move to New York.

Once in New York, in early 1985, she began modelling regularly for *Redline* and *Cosmopolitan*, as well as completing some catalogue work for Macy's and Bloomingdales. In 1986 she got a big break when *Mademoiselle* gave her a contract – she had 20 pages in every issue for five months.

While Stephanie was succeeding in print editorials, her fellow supermodels were also crossing over to work on the catwalk – a move she knew she needed to match. Catwalk was a performance style that seemed daunting initially and she turned down some of her earliest bookings because the thought of posing on a runway platform, in front of a live audience, scared her.

The Paris-based couturier Azzedine Alaïa was the first booking she committed to. For him, her curvaceous figure was ideal to dress. The pair had met originally at the Look of the Year contest – half of the competing models were styled by Kenzō Takada and half by Alaïa. Stephanie wore Kenzō, but had dreamt of being an Alaïa muse.

Alaïa's introduction to distinguished photographers like Richard Avedon helped Stephanie reach the top in the high fashion realm – it was Avedon who shot her debut *Vogue* cover and she would become one of the models he booked most in the latter part of his career.

What made Stephanie super-successful was her ability to pull off both commercial and couture assignments simultaneously – still a rarity at the time. She became the face of Dior and *Playboy*, Versace and Victoria's Secret. It was a juxtaposition that made her ubiquitous in pop culture, beyond just the fashion-industry bubble. →

American *Vogue*, May 1989, photographer Arthur Elgort.

Q&A

with

STEPHANIE SEYMOUR

What originally made you want to pursue modelling?

The idea of being a model was so captivating to me. I was 14 years old and people would always tell me 'You could be a model,' or tell my mother that she should take me to New York. I loved fashion and was very aware of trends – I worshipped Brooke Shields and *Mademoiselle* was my favourite magazine. At the same time, I entered two contests that I had seen in the magazines; one was Elite's Look of the Year and one was to be the [fragrance] Love's Baby Soft girl. It was just something teenage girls did: you sent off the coupon with $20 to enter. But it changed my life and my trajectory forever.

When you started out, you modelled everything from sportswear to evening dresses ...

I really did. From the moment I started to model, I worked every single day. When I first moved to New York, each day would be different – I might work for Macy's, doing furs one day and bras the next, then later in the week I could be doing the cover of a magazine. But, whatever it was that I was doing, I always worked, and it gave me a lot of experience very quickly. I think my story and my beginning is probably pretty common for that time – you worked really hard, and built your portfolio. →

Soon after you started modelling, you got to spend a summer in Paris. What are your memories of the trip?

I remember really just being so scared. I had a great time when I was with my friends, the other young models that I lived with. But I was 15 years old, I hadn't ever gone out on a date and my dad still wouldn't let me get into a car with a boy alone, yet here I was, living in Paris by myself for the summer working on this modelling thing. Even though I was young and it was all a little bit fast for me, I knew it was something that I had to push through. I knew I wasn't going to give up because I felt like fashion was the place for me. I loved the people and the industry immediately, and I still do.

Your first ever catwalk show was with Azzedine Alaïa ...

I was terrified! I can't believe I got out onto the runway because I was in such distress. I was having a complete panic. I remember talking to myself thinking, 'Okay! Walk, turn around.' But he [Alaïa] really took me under his wing – he held me closer and gave me so much love and guidance. Some people would never hire you again, right? He did the opposite. He knew when he hired me that he was choosing someone with no experience, because we had first met when he designed the contestant outfits on Look of the Year. But he didn't care because he loved the way that the dresses looked on me. That was the beginning of a long, beautiful relationship between us.

> " WHEN YOU'RE IN THAT MOMENT AND YOU CREATE SOMETHING THAT IS PURE AND TIMELESS, YOU DO GET A FEELING THAT THIS IS AS GOOD AS IT GETS. "

Was there a point when you found your confidence as a model?

I just always remember thinking that I could do better. Throughout my career, I've never felt like I made it. I just don't have that state of mind. But there have been moments when I've taken amazing photographs with amazing photographers like Richard Avedon or Herb Ritts, and when you're in that moment and you create something that's pure and timeless, you do get a feeling that this is as good as it gets. And that's what keeps you coming back.

HELENA CHRISTENSEN

H
E
L
E
N
A

HELENA
CHRISTENSEN
//

25 December 1968

A career transition from beauty queen to high fashion model should be easy, you might think. Yet the territories of pageanting and catwalk modelling are poles apart, and there are surprisingly few names that have successfully crossed those borders.

Helena Christensen was the supermodel who broke that rule. She was crowned Miss Denmark at the age of 17 and was subsequently contractually obliged to enter the global Miss Universe pageant in Panama – an experience she would later describe as like a 'bootcamp'.

Born to a Peruvian mother and Danish father, Helena grew up in the suburbs of Copenhagen and had a nonchalance that was far better suited to fashion than pageanting. Her passions were photography and travelling – one of her first experiences after finishing school was Greek-island hopping with a friend, working in an Ios bar.

When she came home, she needed some money, so, in September 1987, she entered Elite's Look of the Year contest. Helena was placed in the top 15, but was encouraged to try modelling in Paris, and signed with the agencies Select and Eva.

Once in Paris, her ascent was fast. In 1989 she walked in catwalk shows for Chanel and Dior. Photographer Friedemann Hauss was the first of many to shoot her for French *Elle*. She was styled by Carine Roitfeld in a mosaic of jewellery, then captured by Pamela Hanson riding a bicycle around Paris, wearing wire glasses.

1990 was a pivotal year in fashion, and Helena broke in at its peak. While the established group of supermodels huddled for Peter Lindbergh's lens on the January 1990 cover of British *Vogue*, it was Helena who fronted the March and August issues, solo. →

Karl Lagerfeld decided that the newcomer needed to star in Chanel's next advertising campaign – Helena emerges from an azure swimming pool wearing a dozen-strand pearl necklace, perspex earrings and a swimsuit with a camellia brooch.

'I met Karl the first week I was in Paris as a 20-year-old,' Helena would later tell *Harper's Bazaar*, in 2020. 'He immediately took me under his wing and put me in the legendary Chanel campaign. I was so excited.'

When Miuccia Prada cast Helena in her catwalk show in September 1990, she also decided that she was campaign star material. Helena fronted Prada's debut advertising campaign and was then flown directly from Milan Fashion Week to the island of Capri, where Albert Watson shot her on the rocks.

By the time Helena appeared in the Herb Ritts-directed music video for Chris Isaak's song 'Wicked Games', she was already a key player within the fashion industry. But the role launched her into the pop-culture conversation, just as MTV was reaching its highest-ever audiences.

The video was voted one of the 'sexiest of all time' by viewers, all thanks to Helena's sultry beauty. To Gianni Versace, hers was the 'most beautiful body in fashion'. John Galliano said, 'She fills clothes with life and fire.'

Helena was signed as the new face of Revlon three years into her career, in 1992, and began to appear in group editorials with the supermodels of the day. *The New York Times* decreed that, together, Helena, Linda Evangelista, Naomi Campbell, Claudia Schiffer, Elle Macpherson, Christy Turlington and Cindy Crawford were the 'Magnificent Seven'.

Helena had been a photographer before she became a model, and ultimately sought to further develop her career behind the camera. As always, she set out to defy the expectations of what a beauty queen might do next.

CHRISTY

CHRISTY
TURLINGTON
//

2 January 1969

At Eileen Ford's Manhattan townhouse, aspiring models would bunk up, dormitory-style, under the constant watch and protection of their super-agent. It was a bubble that hundreds of young hopefuls entered when they were first signed with Mrs Ford, and, from her homely base, she would send her 'girls' on an audition-like circuit of 'go-sees' around New York City.

Christy Turlington was at the breakfast table one morning in August 1985, when Ford detailed her schedule of appointments for the day. It included a meeting with a sittings editor, who sent her on to see Arthur Elgort – the photographer who would help launch her career as one of the greatest supermodels of all time.

Christy had been discovered a few years earlier. She was raised in the San Francisco suburbs with her two sisters. Her mother, who was from El Salvador, and father from California, had met in the air – she was a stewardess for Pan Am, he was a pilot. Christy rode horses after school, and, when she was 14, the local photographer Dennie Cody approached her mother at the stables to suggest she could be a model.

She started out posing for catalogue shoots. Christy has braces in many of her earliest photos but was booked to advertise everything from sportswear to bridal gowns. Even once she had signed with the Ford agency in 1984, she still considered modelling to be a temporary gig, and a way to make some pocket money. →

The meeting with Elgort, though, changed that. Elgort identified her as a star, and Christy became his muse – he booked her consistently for American *Vogue*'s inside fashion and beauty pages. Her first *Vogue* cover, however, was shot by Hiro, in March 1986 for *Vogue Italia*. Her second was for British *Vogue* in July 1986 – it was Patrick Demarchelier this time who photographed the newcomer American model wearing the first collection from a new American designer, Donna Karan.

Elle and *Cosmopolitan* shoots followed, and Christy's editorial success soon translated to commercial deals – she fronted adverts for Revlon, Bloomingdales, Missoni and Versace. She became famous internationally as the face of Calvin Klein's Eternity perfume, then signed an exclusive deal as the face of the brand in 1988, which blocked her from working with any other brands or media outlets.

Christy had met Naomi Campbell on her first visit to London in 1985, when the two shot a catalogue for Warehouse together. The job lasted several days, and a lifelong friendship was formed. When Campbell first came to New York, she and Christy shared an apartment. When Linda Evangelista joined their gang, they were known as The Trinity.

As the supermodels became friends and collaborators, they began to work together to boost their collective power. When Christy asked her friend, the hairstylist Oribe, to cut her a bob in 1989, Calvin Klein was reportedly displeased. She used the opportunity to renegotiate her deal, giving her the creative freedom to join some of the exciting artistic group projects her contemporaries were beginning to sign up for.

One of the first that she agreed to was Peter Lindbergh's January 1990 British *Vogue* cover. Christy was at the centre of the swirl of supermodel-dom that followed that picture – but she was one of the first of the group to crave a different kind of lifestyle. In 1994, she stepped back from modelling to study eastern religion and philosophy at New York University. She has dipped her toe back in the water only occasionally since – allowing her primary focus to be the maternal health foundation, Every Mother Counts, which she launched in 2010.

Yves Saint Laurent, Autumn/Winter 1987.

NAOMI

NAOMI
CAMPBELL
//

22 May 1970

There are YouTube tributes and Beyoncé song lyrics dedicated to Naomi Campbell's distinctive runway walk – a straight-backed hip sway, loaded with both elegance and attitude, which she has practised since the 1980s.

Her mother, who was a dancer, inspired her from childhood. A theatre-arts student in London, Naomi was 8 years old when she was selected by the director Don Letts to appear in Bob Marley's 'Is This Love?' music video.

When she was 15, and hanging out after school in Covent Garden, she was approached by Beth Boldt of the modelling agency Synchro. Naomi took the scout's business card and went on some 'go-see' appointments – all without her mother knowing what she was up to.

Her earliest work included shoots for *Company* magazine with photographer Eamonn McCabe, and catwalk shows for Jasper Conran. Martin Brading shot her very first advertising assignment for Richmond-Cornejo, but also gave her a bigger break when he took her to New Orleans for the August 1986 cover of British *Elle*.

From there, Naomi's career went global. Eileen Ford flew to London to sign her. By December, she was living with Christy Turlington in her Manhattan apartment, walking in catwalk shows for Michael Kors and Calvin Klein. She appeared regularly in international *Vogue* editorials. Patrick Demarchelier photographed her in the desert wearing gold Chanel for British *Vogue*'s December 1987 cover. Steven Klein captured her bright-eyed for *Vogue Italia*. →

Naomi's most important and long-lasting friendships were formed in those early days of her career. On one of her first visits to Paris, her purse was stolen in the street. The designer Azzedine Alaïa invited her to stay at his home – he treated her like a daughter and a muse, she called him Papa and learned from watching him work. Aged 16, the Alaïa boutique became her personal closet – she walked in all his shows, as well as for Chanel and Yves Saint Laurent.

Naomi's success in Paris, both on the catwalk and in editorials, was noteworthy. Yet when she sought a French *Vogue* cover in 1988, she was initially turned down. When Naomi told her friend Yves Saint Laurent about the experience, the designer threatened to stop advertising with the magazine if it continued to exclude Black women. Naomi made history as the first Black woman to front French *Vogue* in August 1988.

'I needed to challenge traditional standards of beauty,' she later told British *Vogue*. 'These moments were the result of extra effort – I had to be twice as good.'

Naomi shared in the supermodel experiences that defined 1990, and, like her peers, she became a superstar. The clique stuck together – Linda Evangelista and Christy Turlington famously stood up for Naomi when she experienced racism and was left out of shows and campaigns.

I HAD TO BE TWICE AS GOOD.

Away from the group work, Naomi said yes to many solo projects and leaned into the pop cultural moment perhaps harder than any of her peers. Dubbed 'the reigning megamodel of them all' by *Interview* magazine at the time, she appeared in Michael Jackson's music videos and befriended world leaders. She became as influential socially and politically as she was in fashion.

She was versatile – starring in maximalist advertising campaigns for Gianni Versace, or comparatively subtle imagery for Prada. By 1993 even her falls made world news – when she toppled on the catwalk wearing Vivienne Westwood's platforms, the shoes were bought by the Victoria & Albert Museum in London, and deemed worthy of display.

Naomi's ability to move with the times has been second to none. Perhaps more than any other supermodel from her era, she has developed her career and personal brand to stay, not just relevant, but completely in demand. She became prolific – and still is to this day.

CLAUDIA

CLAUDIA
SCHIFFER
//

25 August 1970

One of fashion's best chance-discovery stories belongs to Claudia Schiffer. Aged 17, she was dancing with friends at the Checker's discothèque in Düsseldorf, Germany, when she was approached by Dominic Galas and Michel Levaton, founder of the Metropolitan Models agency, Paris. Claudia had expressed an interest in working at her father's law firm, but she always loved fashion and she admired her mother's elegant style. Her own look, meanwhile, was 1980s Americana: baggy jeans and oversized sweatshirts.

After her father established that Levaton's offer was genuine, Claudia went to Paris and became a regular booking for French *Elle*, *Vogue* and many other titles. Her first shoot was with photographer Walter Chin. A few weeks later, Gilles Bensimon took her to Mexico where she shot her debut cover.

Around this time, Claudia also met the German photographer Ellen Von Unwerth. One of their earliest stories together was based upon a model's 'off-duty' style. Von Unwerth shot Claudia at the Centre Pompidou, relaxed and wearing her own clothes.

The team at LA denim upstart Guess Jeans saw those images and were inspired to book both the up-and-coming photographer and her muse for their 1989 advertising campaign. Claudia, with her Brigitte Bardot-esque beauty, looking directly down Von Unwerth's lens, symbolized a new strong female gaze within fashion photography. The pictures propelled her to global fame. Claudia – now known as the 'Guess Girl' – was stopped by fans in the street.

Designer Karl Lagerfeld had seen Claudia on the cover of British *Vogue*, shot by Herb Ritts, with a tower of glamorous curled hair. In January 1990 he took a risk, making her the new face of Chanel and casting her in her debut catwalk show. Claudia practised a distinct walk, and smiled naturally for the photographers. She immediately became Lagerfeld's muse, appearing in countless campaigns and catwalk shows, as well as for Chloé, Valentino, Dior and many others throughout the 1990s.

Alongside solo projects, she frequently took part in the era's collaborative shoots. Peter Lindbergh shot the supers wearing Chanel biker boots at the foot of the Brooklyn Bridge for his 'Wild at Heart' American *Vogue* composition. Gianni Versace dressed them to look like rockstars, as he turned his fashion shows into a source of entertainment, and Richard Avedon gathered the band of supers together for Versace's advertising campaigns.

Claudia absorbed it all and applied the skills she learned to a lifetime's worth of varied creative projects – acting, writing, designing, producing and curating. She took her chance that night at the disco, and ran with it. →

Q&A

with

CLAUDIA SCHIFFER

What was your childhood like?

I grew up in a small town near Düsseldorf with three siblings. We were very active, so did ballet, jazz dance and aerobics; I also played the piano and spent a lot of time outdoors playing tennis, swimming in the lakes, and going on forest walks led by my father. My mother was a passionate gardener, so I grew up surrounded by a large garden full of amazing flowers and plants, and I got my love for them from her. I was very shy, but my upbringing gave me a strong sense of family and discipline which helped me navigate the world of fashion.

What are your memories of the day you were discovered?

I was with my best girlfriend Uta and other friends from Hamburg. I remember I was wearing stonewashed Chipie jeans, a Fiorucci sweatshirt and blue eyeshadow. It was the first time I had been to a nightclub in a big city.

What was your reaction when the scout Dominic Galas and the agent Michel Levaton approached you?

I honestly thought it was a joke and suggested that my best friend might be better suited. I remember that encounter so clearly: we were dancing to 'You Spin Me Right Round' by Dead or Alive. However, I took his card and discussed it with my parents the next day. A test shoot was organized, then a few weeks later I found myself in Paris, accompanied by my mother, with a modelling contract negotiated by my father, and the rest is history. →

How did you feel when you first arrived in Paris?

I didn't pack much as I was convinced that once they saw me again they would realize they had made a mistake and send me home! It really was an adventure. Aged 17, I packed my favourite clothes and French school books and set off. In the early weeks, my mother was by my side, showing me how to ride the Métro, coming to photoshoots, meeting the agents, and acting as my chaperone. My father was a lawyer, so he looked over my contracts until I started to understand the business myself. To begin with, I shared a tiny flat with another model from Holland, who was lovely. I lived most of my Parisian 1990s years in Le Marais. I would set off to castings with my portfolio in hand, discovering areas of Paris along the way. I'd eat croissants from across the street and dip them in hot chocolate. I'd also buy herrings from the market and cheese at the fromagerie.

How did you feel when you booked that first *Elle* shoot?

My agent, Aline Soulier, took me to meet Odile Sarron, the casting director of French *Elle*. After introductions and answering a few questions, Sarron asked me to strip back to my underwear. 'Can you do a twirl?' she asked. The very next day, I was booked to do a lingerie shoot in Le Marais with the photographer, Walter Chin. It was 1988. The looks were all white and very pretty and the modelling was naturalistic, so it didn't feel awkward or strange. I soon learnt how to interpret a photographer's direction. Over the following weeks, I was booked for my first location shoot. It was in Cabo San Lucas in Mexico with Elle Macpherson (who was married to the photographer Gilles Bensimon), Rachel Hunter and other models. The article was about French *Elle*'s Stars of Tomorrow and I shot my first cover. It was surreal seeing my image plastered all over Paris kiosks! It was such a great feeling and that's when I realized that I probably wasn't going to be sent home. Up until then, I still thought the agency might realize it had made a mistake.

Chanel was your first catwalk show – what advice did Karl Lagerfeld give you?

Back then, you were mostly either a runway model or you were an editorial model, but the crossover was starting to happen as fashion brands sought out recognizable faces. Chanel was very special. It was the pivotal moment in my career that transformed me from a shy teenager into a supermodel. Karl told me I should just be myself and throughout my career, I've cherished his advice and trusted my instincts.

You have described Karl as your 'magic dust'. How did that moment change your career going forward?

We collaborated for 30 years on countless Chanel campaigns, for numerous fashion magazines and book projects, as well as for his own brand and others. He was one of the few designers, who loved working with muses that inspired him. He invested in them and built a longstanding 'family'. He taught me about fashion, style, image making and also about survival in the fashion business. We travelled the world together and I will be eternally grateful to him.

What moment made you realize that you wanted to pursue this career, in the long term?

At the beginning, modelling was terrifying and exhilarating in equal measures for me and the supermodel fame stretched beyond the catwalk. For that first Guess campaign, I remember flying around the United States to every major city for signings in department stores that attracted huge crowds and appearing on all the major TV shows – from David Letterman and Jay Leno to Oprah. It was insane: like being a rockstar. One morning, back in my apartment block in New York, near Central Park, sleepy eyed and with bed hair, I rode the elevator, and someone asked, 'Are you the Guess girl?!' I knew then my life had changed forever.

> " CHANEL WAS VERY SPECIAL. IT WAS THE PIVOTAL MOMENT IN MY CAREER THAT TRANSFORMED ME FROM A SHY TEENAGER INTO A SUPERMODEL. "

Yves Saint Laurent, Autumn/Winter 1991.

YASMEEN

YASMEEN
GHAURI
//

23 March 1971

Yasmeen Ghauri quit her job at a McDonald's near Montreal when she was 17. She was finishing school and had been working in the fast-food chain while she decided what to do about university – she was 'employee of the month' at the time she resigned.

Her local hairdresser, Edward Zaccaria, was the one who had suggested that she could be a model and had given her the contact information for the agent Giovanni Bernadi. After one meeting, she signed with Bernadi – and (unusually for the industry) she stuck with him for her entire career.

Yasmeen's German mother and Pakistani father were supportive, but, initially, her father had concerns. She had grown up in an Islamic household – he was a traditionalist and a cleric in Quebec's Muslim community.

Pursuing modelling would go against his wishes for her.

For the first six months after signing with Bernadi, Yasmeen attended castings in Montreal, which had a thriving local catalogue industry. Yasmeen, however, was mostly rejected. The racism and prejudice she experienced were just as she had suffered all her life, growing up in a predominantly white neighbourhood.

When she first went to Europe in the spring of 1990, however, she was an immediate success. She found fame on the catwalk for her unique hip movements – her attitude-packed strut appealed to Gianni Versace, who was one of the first to hire her, followed swiftly by Azzedine Alaïa and Karl Lagerfeld at Chanel. In her first Yves Saint Laurent show, she wore a slinky black slip skirt with a bralette and caught media attention. →

Yasmeen's walk was unique – *The New York Times* called it a 'ball-bearing swivel of her hips', and Karl Lagerfeld commented that she had 'invented a new way to walk that a lot of girls are trying to imitate.'

By January 1991, Yasmeen had three French and American *Elle* covers to her name, a Chanel advertisement and had starred in an Elton John music video. She added campaigns for Dior, Anne Klein and Jil Sander to her portfolio.

Her work for Victoria's Secret was also influential. She was signed in 1992 as a face of the brand, fronting what was then a booming catalogue business, with her pictures being posted out to households all over America.

To mark American *Vogue*'s 100th anniversary issue, she posed for Patrick Demarchelier with Claudia Schiffer, Naomi Campbell, Tatjana Patitz, Christy Turlington, Linda Evangelista, Cindy Crawford, Niki Taylor, Elaine Irwin and Karen Mulder, forming a stack of supermodels.

Unlike her peers, though, Yasmeen resisted the term 'supermodel'. She avoided publicity and turned down party invitations and interviews. On the rare occasion she would agree to comment, she would remind reporters that the job was a temporary one for her.

'When people say "What is it like to be a supermodel?", I just think it's such a stupid label,' she told a local Canadian newspaper in 1992. 'It's like saying "What does it feel like to be a top businessman, a super-businessman?"'

In 1997, at the age of 26, Yasmeen formally announced her retirement from modelling. She was at the top of the game, in an era where models were beginning to push the supposed 'age limits' in the profession – but she wanted a new experience.

'I went from school to work, so I didn't have the opportunity to explore my interests and decide what I wanted to do,' she said when she was interviewed for E! network's 'Model' documentary series. 'Now, I want to discover myself.'

EVA
HERZIGOVÁ
//

10 March 1973

Competing with the boys was the priority for Eva Herzigová as a child growing up in the mountain villages of Litvínov. She has described sports as being like a religion at home in 1980s communist Czechoslovakia, and she set out to prove herself at cross-country skiing, skateboarding, windsurfing, tree-climbing and more.

She was 16 years old when, in 1989, she entered a modelling competition in Prague, organized by the Parisian agency Metropolitan Models. Eva hadn't intended to be there – she was accompanying a friend who had wanted to enter. The organizers instead chased her down a hallway, begging her to take part, too. She accepted, and was crowned the winner of the entire contest, beating more than 400 entrants and earning the prize of a ticket to Paris.

Then she had to tell her parents. The opportunity for Eva to work abroad for three months, when many of her relatives had never left Czechoslovakia, both excited and scared her. Her mother, a secretary, was hesitant, but her father, an electrician, insisted she should go.

'He said "This is her white horse,"' Eva recalled in a 2019 interview with Tatler. '"This is her opportunity to get out."'

It took six months to get permission from the Czech government to go. Two months after Eva arrived in Paris, the Velvet Revolution brought about the collapse of communism in her home country, opening up the possibility of travel for all, as well as a long-term career as an international supermodel for her. →

Eva's first few months in Paris were filled with 'go-sees' and test shoots. She navigated her way around the city, attending up to 12 castings per day.

Azzedine Alaïa was responsible for one of her breakthrough appearances – he cast her in her first major catwalk show, in September 1991. More shows followed and she became a favourite at Chanel and Valentino.

By January 1992, Eva was on the cover of British *Vogue* in a group portrait named 'fresh faces'. Peter Lindbergh shot the composition in which Eva wears draped white jersey, standing shoulder to shoulder with Beverly Peele, Petra Lindblad, Nadja Auermann and Claudia Mason.

When Ellen Von Unwerth cast her as the next 'Guess Girl' in 1992, the photographer played on the fact that journalists had dubbed Eva as a modern answer to Marilyn Monroe. In the adverts, Eva's beauty looks almost vintage, amplified via styling her hair in set curls and painting her lips bright red.

Working with Guess was a huge deal in fashion advertising at the time – the relatively new denim company was getting used to making global headlines with its campaigns. But, three years into her career, Eva would be immortalized in fashion and advertising history for another attention-grabbing advert.

Ahead of Valentine's Day 1994, the Canada-based brand Wonderbra sought to promote its push-up bras in the United Kingdom. Executive Trevor Beattie signed up Von Unwerth, who asked Eva to model. The 'Hello Boys' campaign was launched, becoming simultaneously one of the most controversial and successful marketing concepts of all time.

Prior to the campaign, lingerie advertisements had mostly featured discreetly inside women's magazines. Now, Eva's image was displayed on vast billboards. The pictures were a distraction to drivers, according to reports at the time.

A global conversation was sparked as to whether the messaging was feminist or sexist. Either way, Wonderbra sold over one million bras and the commercial was deemed one of the most memorable and successful in history. Above all, it confirmed Eva's super-selling power.

Hervé Leger, Autumn/Winter 1993.

T Y R A

TYRA **BANKS**
//
4 December 1973

As Tyra Banks understood, the business of model discovery could itself be a source of entertainment. Tyra launched her reality television format, *America's Next Top Model*, in 2003. But the idea for it came at the start of her own career in the late 1980s – her generation of supermodels gained popularity and notoriety, and with that came interest in their roots and how they got there.

Tyra was raised in Inglewood, California. Her mother was a medical photographer but took headshots for aspiring models on the side. At 12 years old, acting as her assistant, Tyra would have witnessed dozens of hopefuls. It hadn't occurred to her that she too might like to model, though, until a classmate at school suggested it.

At 15, Tyra asked her mother to snap a set of photos for her, which she took to agencies around Los Angeles. She signed first with LA Models and did local adverts for Macy's in the *Los Angeles Times*. She made plans to study film at Loyola Marymount – but deferred her entry for a year.

When an agent from Elite in Paris came to town, seeking new faces to take to the upcoming Paris Fashion Week, she picked Tyra's picture off the agency's headshot wall. Tyra rose to the opportunity, visiting the local library at the Fashion Institute of Design Merchandising to watch old runway tapes and study how other models walked. She practised her signature walk with the help of the librarian. →

'She sat me down and showed me the right way to look at the photos to determine the aesthetic of each designer,' Tyra later told the website LeanIn. 'Two weeks later, I found myself pounding the pavement in Paris. Before each "go-see", I would change things up: for Chanel, it was flat-ironed hair and smoky eyes. For Yves Saint Laurent, it was hair slicked back in a bun and bright red lipstick.'

Tyra booked an unprecedented 25 shows on her debut Paris Fashion Week. Her popularity amongst European designers was instant – she would later tell Howard Stern, in 2011, that she could earn $50,000 a day on the catwalks in Paris and Milan.

Perhaps because of her popularity with the major fashion houses in Europe, but also because of the general obsession with celebrity models in the early 1990s, Tyra quickly became famous. The tabloid press repeatedly cast her as a rival to Naomi Campbell, whose profile was also on the rise. The commentary was inaccurate and racist, both women would later say.

Tyra went on to gain big bookings both in the advertising and editorial spheres – campaigns for Ralph Lauren and covers for *Elle* magazine. In 1995 she signed a multi-year deal with Cover Girl Cosmetics.

In 1996 she became the first African American woman to star on the cover of *GQ* magazine. A year later, she made history again, on the cover of *Sports Illustrated*, and was the first Black woman to front the Victoria's Secret catalogue, too.

Tyra's supermodel USP was her 'smize' – the way she could expressively use her eyes to follow her smile. But it was also her personality. She was bubbly and telegenic, straddling a career as an actor and a presenter alongside her modelling work from as early as 1993, when she first got a part in the cult series *The Fresh Prince of Bel Air*. As supermodels became cultural figures, she joined in wholeheartedly, appearing in music videos for Tina Turner and Michael Jackson.

She had long harboured ambitions to become a television producer and jumped at the opportunity to create, produce and host *America's Next Top Model*. While she stopped modelling full time, her career diversified greatly, with more acting and talk-show hosting, as well as releasing music and authoring fiction. Tyra took the concept of a 'model as mogul' to new heights.

KATE **MOSS**
//

16 January 1974

The Storm agency founder, Sarah Doukas, was in the air when she first approached the teenager who would become her most famous discovery.

She had noticed Kate Moss at New York's John F. Kennedy Airport. Kate was with her father – who worked for Pan Am – waiting on standby to get a flight home to London. Once onboard, Doukas went over to introduce herself as soon as the seatbelt signs were turned off. Kate was a girl – just 14 – and shorter than the glamorous and curvaceous supermodels who were ruling in 1988. But Doukas predicted that the fashion industry would crave a new look soon enough, and, in Kate, she could see a sort of anti-supermodel.

In the days after she took Doukas's details, Kate's mother took her to Storm's London office and agreed to let her sign with the agency. She was still at school, so her career started slowly, during the holidays. →

Some of the first photographers that Kate was sent to were simply not interested. The powerful personalities that were ruling the catwalks could be seen all over the papers, and partying with George Michael. Surely nothing else would sell?

But Kate represented a new, young, grunge scene in London – and the up-and-coming photographer Corinne Day could see her potential.

Day, who was herself a former model, took Kate over to her grandmother's home where she had grown up, and took test shots in the garden to shape her raw talent.

Knowing that *Vogue* and *Harper's Bazaar* were only interested in the 'glamazons', she pitched her protégé to Phil Bicker, editor of underground magazine *The Face*.

In July 1990, Day shot the editorial that launched Kate's career – a cover of *The Face*, capturing the concept of a new, young 'Summer of Love'. A small crew, including stylist Melanie Ward, had decamped from London to the gritty beaches of Camber Sands. When so much else in fashion was about maximalism and excess, the lo-fi shots revealed Kate as a natural beauty.

The pictures were controversial even at the time – here was a teenager, topless and smoking. Her name was launched in the industry, and she did more work for *The Face*, as well as being cast in some group adverts for Versace.

The art director Fabien Baron, who worked on Calvin Klein's advertising campaigns, saw those early images of Kate, and likened her potential impact on youth culture to that of Twiggy. →

Klein commissioned Herb Ritts to shoot his autumn 1992 television commercial and print adverts, hiring Kate to pose in just her Calvin Klein jeans, wrapping her arms around actor Mark Wahlberg.

The provocative pictures were commented on globally, and Kate's name was at the centre of discussion about the 'new waif' and 'heroin chic' beauty trends.

In the United Kingdom, The 'Cool Britannia' movement was launched in entertainment – and Kate was the fashion industry's poster girl. By March 1993, Day had shot her for the cover of British *Vogue* under the tagline 'fashion's new spirit'. Their anti-glam was now the global mainstream's biggest trend.

As her career developed, Kate became one of the most in-demand supermodels of her generation – she stopped the fashion wheel and turned it in a whole new direction. She was embraced by the maximalist designers such as Versace, and joined the glossy supermodel clique, but could also do gritty or ethereal beauty for Alexander McQueen or *i-D* magazine.

As Kate became famous, so did her discovery story. Reporters revelled in the fairytale of the seemingly ordinary girl, plucked from obscurity in the London suburb of Croydon, who became a supermodel. Hers became a fashion fable – probably the most retold of all time.

AMBER
VALLETTA
//

9 February 1974

AMBER

In a Paris apartment in 1992, two stylists worked simultaneously to chop off Amber Valletta's hair. The 18-year-old didn't know it, but the decision to ask Yannick d'Is and Ward Stegerhoek to give her a new edgy crop would land her an American *Vogue* cover – the first of 17, and counting.

Amber found herself in France because her agency, Ford, had just opened a new office in Paris. Her bookings were steady – Guerlain beauty adverts and Claude Montana fashion shows, with a cover of French *Elle* to her name, too. But the haircut was set to accelerate things for the teenager from Oklahoma.

Amber was born in Phoenix, Arizona, but grew up in Tulsa. She loved to perform, and when she was 15 her mother paid for classes at the Linda Layman modelling school, to give her an outlet.

The local agency had affiliations with Ford, and in 1989 a scout from Italy came to visit. He selected Amber and one other student to go to Milan for the summer – the other girl's mother played chaperone, as Amber's mother worked in a postal office and couldn't take the time off. She arrived in Milan with Polaroids and left with a portfolio full of test shots and editorials for small magazines, many by Fabrizio Ferri.

She had found some success in Paris, but after having her hair cut, she was booked for almost every major runway show for the rest of the year – jobs from Prada ready-to-wear to Valentino couture. →

American *Vogue*'s editors were curious about the designers' new-found 'girl of the moment' and booked Amber and a fellow newcomer, Canadian Shalom Harlow, for a shoot with Arthur Elgort on the coast in Santa Monica. She and Harlow posed with a picnic basket and drove a classic car, but it was Elgort's portrait of Amber in a ruffled collar and a beret that made the February 1993 cover.

Back in New York, she shared an apartment with Harlow, who became her best friend, and the new girl in town Kate Moss came over to hang out. As a trio, Moss, Harlow and Amber could epitomize the waif look in editorials while keeping up with their glossy, famous peers at parties. They were described in the press as the second wave of supermodels.

The key to Amber's initial success, but also her longevity in the industry, was her versatility. From the outset, she showed that range – she could do raw, bed-head beauty for Calvin Klein's Escape fragrance adverts, or glowing Italian glamour for Gianni Versace. When she launched Tom Ford's new era at Gucci, opening his catwalk show in 1995, she was powerful and sexy.

By 1996 Amber sought to diversify her career, hosting MTV's *House of Style* and eventually pursuing acting, too. Today, over three decades into her career, she picks her assignments on her own terms, choosing typically to work with brands that champion sustainable fashion. →

with

AMBER VALLETTA

You went to modelling school – what did you learn there?
I was such a performer, my mom thought I needed an outlet. There was an agency in my hometown that had a school attached and they taught us how to walk on the runway. I remember I felt so silly because I didn't have a super-elegant walk yet. They also taught us to mannequin model – I wish we did this today! You stand on a box in a store, and you strike a position like a mannequin. You hold it for three minutes then you change positions robotically – pop it and lock it. I did this at my local mall, it was one of the first jobs I got paid for.

Your success came gradually – was that important for your longevity?
I learned very early on how to show up for work and be a professional. You started with smaller magazines and worked your way up. There was time to develop and build. You would get discovered by bigger photographers and designers as you gained some experience. It's very different today – models often become famous instantly. →

Let's talk about the haircut …

That haircut changed my career overnight. I was still a teenager, but I had this very classic ladylike bob that curled under. People thought I looked a lot older than I was. I met the hairdresser Yannick d'Is and I asked him to cut it. It wasn't planned – no agency told me to do it. We were thinking of an old 1960s shot. Nobody had the haircut, and it became the epitome of 'the waif'.

What was the camaraderie like between you and your peers?

We needed each other back then in a way that most people can't understand. Imagine any group of people being in a pressure-cooker situation, but we were extremely young and in the spotlight. It was like being in a girl band or on a Disney show. We were kids and we didn't go to university; we had our own sorority which was the fashion industry. We needed each other to survive.

> **" WE WERE EXTREMELY YOUNG AND IN THE SPOTLIGHT. IT WAS LIKE BEING IN A GIRL BAND OR ON A DISNEY SHOW. "**

With hindsight, which moments early in your career felt particularly special and defining?

I've had pinch-me moments in my life, but I never stopped to think about it like that. I'm not that kind of person. I think, though, when you get those big milestones it is super exciting, like the first cover of American *Vogue*. Or opening the Tom Ford Gucci show; I'll never forget that. Even I had goosebumps when the lights came on and I started walking – there was this energy surge in the room. Fashion shows like that feel like theatre.

ALEK **WEK**
//
16 April 1977

A single Polaroid picture, taken at a fair in London's Crystal Palace Park in 1995, launched Alek Wek's career. The snapper was Fiona Ellis, a scout for the agency Models One. After Kate Moss's chance-discovery story had made world news, an agent never left home without a camera.

Alek was an 18-year-old art foundation student at the London College of Fashion. By this point, she had lived in Britain for four years, but her birthplace was Wau, in what is now South Sudan. Alek, her mother, and her eight siblings had been forced to flee conflict in their hometown in 1991 – her father had died a few months previously. 'We had an extremely simple life. No running water, no electricity,' she told *The Guardian* in 2014. 'We had no idea how poor we were, because we were so rich in our culture, our education.'

After she was spotted in the street, Alek's first job was not an editorial, but a 1995 music video: Tina Turner was shooting the new James Bond theme song for *GoldenEye*. Alek attended the casting with just that Polaroid, in lieu of an accomplished portfolio. Still, she was booked, and gazed at a Bond-worthy giant diamond for the assignment.

She now had a talking point on her resume. In the summer holidays of 1996, she flew to New York to test the waters, with a plan to return to university and take a design degree at Central Saint Martins in the autumn. →

That plan didn't work out; instead, she signed with Ford. By September, she found herself booked by Ralph Lauren, Donna Karan and Calvin Klein at New York Fashion Week.

Alek brought joy and energy to the pages of *Vogue Italia*'s October issue, under the direction of Steven Meisel. François Nars asked her to appear in his first cosmetics advertising campaign. Then Lee Alexander McQueen claimed Alek as a muse – first, he hired her for Givenchy couture, and then for his eponymous brand. One season he might envision her with a blonde mullet, the next in gold body paint.

'I had just been discovered when Lee requested me,' Alek later told *Vogue* in 2019. 'I remember looking in the mirror with the blonde hair and that outfit for the autumn 1997 show and thinking, "Wow!" That is why I love what I do, because these designers dress you in ways that you would never imagine.'

In the realm of editorial, Alek became a regular *Elle* girl. She got her debut American *Elle* cover in November 1997, becoming the first African model to front the magazine, and she was styled by Gilles Bensimon in a white Armani jacket. The cover was hugely impactful, challenging the misconception that a woman with dark skin wouldn't sell magazines. Fans wrote to the editors to praise her 'proud and radiant' beauty.

More covers inevitably followed, as did more music videos, and industry accolades – Alek was named MTV's Model of the Year in 1997.

Perhaps the most telling measure of her influence, though, was summed up by the Oscar-winning actress Lupita Nyong'o. In a speech she made for the Essence Black Women in Hollywood Awards, in 2014, she described how she felt when, as a young woman, she first saw Alek achieving supermodel feats in the media.

'She was dark as night; she was on all of the runways and in every magazine and everyone was talking about how beautiful she was …' Nyong'o said. 'When I saw Alek, I inadvertently saw a reflection of myself. Now, I had a spring in my step because I felt more seen, more appreciated.'

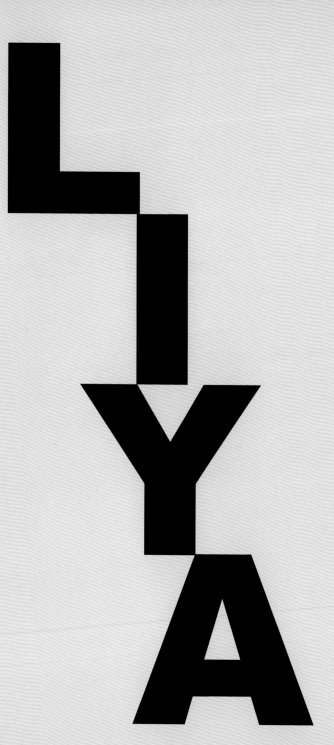

LIYA
KEBEDE
//
1 March 1978

As actresses like Jennifer Aniston and Gwyneth Paltrow began to claim the sought-after spots on fashion magazine covers at the end of the 1990s, the parameters of what made a model turn 'super' were shifting.

Liya Kebede matched up to every checklist, old and new. She appeared on three American *Vogue* print covers, yes, but also hit the new marks, becoming one of the first to win the Model of the Year accolade on the industry website Models.com, which launched in 1999, as well as featuring on *Forbes*'s annual list of highest earners, which started in 2000.

Born and raised in Addis Ababa, Ethiopia, Liya had posters of Naomi Campbell stuck to her bedroom wall as a teenager. Her mother worked in public relations and her father was a manager with Ethiopian Airlines – Liya and her four brothers were raised to be bookish.

Liya attended the French school Lycée Guebre-Mariam and, along with some classmates, modelled a little in charity fashion shows and for local boutiques. In one of these shows, she was noticed by a French film director, who put her in touch with an agent in Paris.

After she had finished school, she first went to Paris for three months. When she felt homesick, though, she changed her plans and went to live with her brother in Chicago, signing with Elite's regional office there. For a couple of years, Liya mostly booked local catalogue work – aside from one show for Ralph Lauren during New York Fashion Week in 1999.

Then, the New York casting director James Scully spotted her comp (business) card while in town for a meeting. He couldn't believe that Liya was 'stuck there' doing commercials in Chicago, and sent some Polaroids of her to designer Tom Ford, via Fed Ex. Three days later Ford called him with the instruction to book her exclusively. →

Appearing in Ford's Gucci show in February 2000 was a breakthrough moment for Liya and she received several job opportunities off the back of the appearance. As it happened, Liya was three months pregnant, expecting her first child with her husband.

She completed shoots for *i-D* and American *Vogue*, before taking some maternity leave. When she returned to work, Ford backed her again, signing her as the face of Yves Saint Laurent for spring 2002 with a campaign photographed by Steven Meisel. (Between 1999 and 2004, Ford was the creative director at both Gucci and Yves Saint Laurent.) She also appeared on the catwalk for Christian Dior Couture, Alexander McQueen, Celine and others.

The new editor of French *Vogue*, Carine Roitfeld, was another early, and very enthusiastic, fan. In May 2002, she dedicated an entire issue to Liya, commissioning Inez & Vinoodh to shoot a portfolio of editorials allowing Liya to show her range. The 'All About Liya' cover called her 'our fashion heroine'.

When Liya was announced as the face of Estée Lauder in 2003 (the first Ethiopian woman to sign such a contract), as well as the face of GAP, Louis Vuitton and Tiffany & Co., it was clear that her look was magnetic for brands at all levels of the market.

She shied away from publicity, which arguably made her more appealing to the designers who wanted to keep the focus on their collections. But, at the same time, she impressed the mass audiences with her other moves – acting and creating a foundation in her name at the height of her fame, with a mission to reduce maternal and newborn mortality in Ethiopia.

Harper's Bazaar would later dub her approach a 'quiet revolution'.

KAREN

KAREN **ELSON**
//
14 January 1979

On Karen Elson's 18th birthday, she had her eyebrows shaved off. Her mousey red hair was given a cherry dye-job and cut into a spiky bob. Karen was living at Eileen Ford's townhouse in New York and the old-school agent Mrs Ford was worried that Karen's new punk look might put off some of the more classic couture clients.

None of that mattered, though, because the makeover had happened on a career-defining Steven Meisel shoot for *Vogue Italia*. The pictures would ultimately launch Karen as a supermodel, validating years of hard work and personal turmoil in the run-up.

Prior to that 1997 editorial, Karen had been close to giving up on her dream and returning to England. She had grown up in the northeastern town of Oldham and was severely bullied as a teen. Reading fashion and music magazines was a form of escapism for her – she liked musicians Nick

Cave and Robert Smith for their gothic style as much as their emotive lyrics.

When she was 15, she went to an open casting call with Boss Model Management in Manchester. The founder, Debra Burns, spotted her unusual beauty and her potential, even though she was nothing like the regional catalogue girls the agency might usually sign. As soon as Karen finished school at 16, Burns sent her on the train down to London to start attending castings. Despite making a friend for life in fellow future supermodel Erin O'Connor, she had very little luck.

Karen needed to earn some money and did what so many other hopeful British models were doing at the time: she went to Tokyo for a few months. A stint in Japan or Singapore could typically help an aspiring model to get some practice and build a portfolio – as well as to earn. Karen packed in up to three catalogue shoots per day. →

Signing with the Ford agency, and relocating to New York, Karen was hopeful about giving modelling one last chance. If nothing big happened, she figured she would return home and perhaps pursue a career as an air stewardess (her school's career counsellor had suggested it, when Karen said that her ambition was to travel).

But the February 1997 *Vogue Italia* cover changed it all. With Meisel photographing, Pat McGrath on makeup and Ward on hair, Karen's beauty was transformed and her potential range as a model was exposed.

Catwalk bookings for Alexander McQueen, Prada and Jean Paul Gaultier followed, then adverts for Versace. Karen won Model of the Year at the VH1 Fashion Awards.

In editorials, she showed how she could evolve her look. Arthur Elgort shot her as an avant-garde Victorian queen across 12 pages in British *Vogue*. For photographer Jean-Baptiste Mondino she became more of a retro redhead, with a set wave and shiny scarlet lip gloss, making the cover of French *Vogue*. She joined the next generation of supermodels for group portraits – Karen walked arm-in-arm with Gisele Bündchen, Maggie Rizer and Audrey Marnay in American *Vogue*'s September 1998 issue, and appeared alongside fellow Brits Erin O'Connor and Jade Parfitt for the cover of *Vogue Italia*.

She could channel punk, vintage glamour, otherworldly etherealness or a hard edge – adapting her look to suit the vision of any designer or photographer, crucially without ever losing the sense of herself. Karen became known as a beauty chameleon – and she was never sent back to Oldham. →

Q&A

with

KAREN ELSON

Tell us how it all began for you?

The beauty ideal in northern England when I was growing up was Pamela Anderson on *Baywatch,* or Cindy Crawford. So, I was really bullied for how I looked. A girl at school, though, one day said, 'You could be a model.' I thought, 'That's wild!' It planted a seed, and I went home to look in the Yellow Pages and the classified ads in the back of my *Just 17* magazine. I found that there was a model agency in Manchester called Boss Models. I decided that I needed to meet the founder, Debbie Burns. I called and they said occasionally they did open castings. I hung up and was so nervous that I did nothing for probably another year after.

What eventually gave you the courage to pursue the opportunity?

I didn't have any friends. That time of my life was so difficult and painful that just to have something to look forward to during the summer holidays, I gave them a call again. They had an open house, and I got the train to Manchester and did the casting call. I wore a black satin dress that I'd saved my pocket money for from Topshop. I'd never done anything like it before, but I think inside I just knew that where I grew up was not where I was going to end up. In the room full of 40 or so people, I was the one she picked.

You took control of your own future ...

I don't think I've ever really told the full story before. I've always been quite evasive when people have asked me about how I was discovered, I think because I didn't want to be disrespectful to my family. But I was desperate to escape Oldham.

What were some of your first experiences as a model?

For the first year, I was essentially Debra Burns's intern. She knew I was an unusual case – I was really young as well, so she

was, thankfully, quite protective of me and gave me some valuable work experience. I would send cheques to the bank, photocopy things, and walk her dog, Pooch. When I left school at 16, I was straight on the train to London to start doing castings. Nothing was really happening for me, so I went to Tokyo to earn some money – it was the common thing to do back then, if you weren't born with a silver spoon in your mouth.

You were on the verge of quitting modelling, but then you met Steven Meisel …
I can't stress enough how close to giving up I was. Everybody around me was saying, 'You can't do this anymore.' I went to New York – I think I had about £20 to my name. The pressure was mounting to come home and get a real job. Then I met Steven, and, thank God, it went well. He just understood the weird little girl. He got me.

Your *Vogue Italia* cover launched your career – what are your memories of the day?
It was my 18th birthday and they shaved my eyebrows off. I went back to Eileen Ford's house where I was living, and I remember her panicking. I have to give her so much credit because she really did look after her girls and keep us safe back then. But I went to my room, and I remember looking in the mirror and thinking 'Yeah, that's who I am. I feel like myself.' It was the most playful, inventive and creative shoot and I felt I was being seen for the first time as an artist.

> " A GIRL AT SCHOOL … ONE DAY SAID, 'YOU COULD BE A MODEL.' I THOUGHT, 'THAT'S WILD!' IT PLANTED A SEED. "

GISELE
BÜNDCHEN
//

20 July 1980

GISELE

The era of the supermodels was over. Or was it? Just as the fashion industry's obsession with anonymous beauty and edgy 'heroin chic' was peaking, along came Gisele Bündchen.

Her success wasn't instant – to turn the tide in fashion required resilience.

Gisele's first experience as a model came at the age of 14. She and two of her five sisters had enrolled in a modelling course in their hometown of Horizontina, Brazil, enticed by the fact that the course ended with a trip to São Paulo – a big city that they hadn't visited before.

They were in a mall, chaperoned by their mother, when a scout from the agency Elite approached Gisele. She had been enjoying experiences like eating her first McDonald's and visiting an amusement park. She was dressed in a black uniform, the same as the 54 other girls on the trip.

Her parents allowed her to do a test portfolio, and in September she entered Elite's Look of the Year contest. She was placed second nationally and fourth globally at the final, which was held in Ibiza, Spain. Despite not winning, she was one of five contestants selected to move to São Paulo to model full time.

In January 1995, Gisele took that chance and left home forever – only to be mugged on arrival in São Paulo for the cash that her father had lent to cover her first month of living away.

Gisele shared an apartment with several older models – they went out partying while she studied and worked. She would attend castings and face rejection daily – judged for her distinct face, and the shape of her nose. She was told at times, in no uncertain terms, that she would never make the cover of a magazine. →

Initially, she shot Japanese catalogues and Brazilian teen magazines. She cuddled a toy leopard on her debut cover, for the teen title *Capricho*.

Steadily, she made it into the pages of Brazilian *Marie Claire* and *Vogue Brasil*. Then she knew it was time to try the runway in New York. Her first trip there was in 1996 and, despite pacing to 'go-sees' all over the city on foot and on the subway, she booked just two shows – for Carolina Herrera and Oscar de la Renta.

When she was 16, she relocated to New York permanently and tried more to find work with international clients. At the next round of shows, in February 1997, Giorgio Armani was one of the few who cast her.

Gisele's breakthrough came that September when, after being rejected by 42 other designers, Lee Alexander McQueen chose her for his latest London Fashion Week show. The concept was typically artistic and provoking – models wore white and walked under a shower, causing their clothes to become see-through and their makeup to dissolve. Gisele wore a painted-on tube top, and faux tears of black mascara ran down her cheeks.

That McQueen appearance was influential, and other designers began to take notice. Dolce & Gabbana and Versace catwalks followed swiftly – by the end of 1998 she had done 85 shows and scored campaigns for Chloé, Missoni and Valentino.

All the experience she had gained previously shooting editorials paid off, too – she shot for American *Elle*, her first international cover for British *Marie Claire* and a December *i-D* cover that namechecked her 'A Girl Called Gisele'.

In less than six months, aged 19, she appeared on the cover of American *Vogue* for the first time, under the banner 'The Return of the Sexy Model'. It was becoming increasingly rare to see a new model launched at this level, as actresses began to be routinely profiled for the magazine, taking the prestigious cover spots once owned solely by models.

How did Gisele follow up the feat? By appearing on the magazine's November and December covers that year too.

Gisele brought healthy figures, curves and muscles back into style, and understood wellness as a new frontier within fashion, long before it was a mainstream trend.

The girl who was rejected became one of the most successful supermodels of all time – and the *Forbes*-accredited highest paid in the world for a record 15 years in a row.

NATALIA

NATALIA
VODIANOVA
//

28 February 1982

On an Air France economy flight from Moscow to Paris in 1999, Natalia Vodianova was enjoying the best meal of her life. She had a piece of Camembert, pasta, and a chocolate brownie for dessert. 'It was by far the best food I'd ever had,' she later recalled on her YouTube channel. 'At the time, I had never tried anything like it.'

Natalia grew up in Nizhny Novgorod, an industrial city in western Russia. She began working at the age of 11, selling fruit at her mother's street stall, while juggling school and caring for her sister who had autism. At the age of 15, tired of being confronted by her mother's aggressive creditors, she separated from her and set up a fruit stand of her own.

'Sometimes we had incredible days where we could buy meat, but then a bad day would come and we would basically be left with nothing,' she said of the experience.

When she was 16, she started dating a boy who was enrolled in a modelling school. He encouraged her and paid for her to attend some classes, too – the lessons included posing and poetry. After three months, in April 1999, there was a casting. Natalia made a miniskirt to wear by cutting up her grandmother's clothes, as the organizers had suggested it was what all applicants needed to wear.

'The casting was horrible,' she remembered. 'All the girls had to line up wearing their skimpy clothes. I refused to stand in the line, hid in the corner and watched what was happening. Then someone came up to me and took my picture.' →

It was the model scout Alexei Vasiliev. He helped Natalia to sign with the Paris agency Viva. By the time Natalia left her hometown for Paris, her mother was in debt and on the verge of losing her home. Her first agent wrote her a cheque for $5,000 to save her family and allow her a fresh start.

On arriving in Paris, Natalia started to learn English. Her career ascended, with editorials for French *Elle*, Australian *Marie Claire* and *Teen Vogue*.

Almost as quickly, she fell in love and married, in November 2001, when she was 19 years old and eight months pregnant. She continued modelling throughout her pregnancy – most famously Juergen Teller photographed her lying on the beach for a Marc Jacobs advertising campaign, with her stomach rising above the sand dunes.

Having proven her ability to take provocative pictures, Natalia turned her attention to making an impact on the catwalk. Just weeks after giving birth, in February 2002, she returned to the runway and had her breakthrough season, opening and closing Tom Ford's show at Yves Saint Laurent, as well as walking for Alexander McQueen, Gucci and Stella McCartney.

A Gucci fragrance campaign was shot, then more deals with L'Oréal, Calvin Klein and Louis Vuitton were signed. The press nicknamed Vodianova 'Supernova'.

She was selected for a range of editorials, depicting different styles – her face was painted into a metallic heart shape for Sølve Sundsbø's lens at *Numéro*, while for Michael Thompson's *W* magazine anniversary shoot, she wore a red tiered gown amongst her supermodel colleagues, including Naomi Campbell, Kate Moss, Christy Turlington, Gisele Bündchen and Iman.

If a pictorial might best summarize Natalia's fairytale success story, it could be the time she was cast as a couture Alice in Wonderland for American *Vogue*'s December 2003 issue. In the blockbuster shoot, styled by Grace Coddington and lensed by Annie Leibovitz, Natalia is Alice and wears blue dresses by Tom Ford, Marc Jacobs and Donatella Versace, with the designers themselves dressed up beside her. At this point, fashion was her world – and she was the main character.

ASHLEY

A S H L E Y
GRAHAM
//
30 October 1987

The curve modelling industry traditionally operated as a sideline to mainstream fashion. A handful of women – like Sophie Dahl, Emme and Kate Dillon – had made it into the mass fashion magazines in the 1990s and early 2000s. But Ashley Graham was the first to become a household name and a supermodel.

There is a trophy, still on display at her mother's house in Nebraska, that symbolizes the moment it all started for the changemaker. Her award? The Top Plus-size Model at an expo in Texas in the year 2000. Ashley was 13.

She was scouted at a mall in Nebraska a year before winning it. A Kansas City talent agent, Clark Cordova from I & I Models, approached her, when she was with her father.

She enrolled in a $2,000 modelling course – her mother drove her three hours each way, weekly, for six months, to allow her to pursue the opportunity.

The day after the convention, Ashley was signed by the Wilhelmina agency. Despite her age, her first job was with local department store Pamida, modelling bras. Her mother made them sign a piece of paper promising to airbrush out her nipples.

While still at school, she modelled for Macy's and Nordstrom, Walmart bra boxes, and Jennifer Lopez's clothing line JLo (the latter she has described as a highlight, as she received free velvet tracksuits). She switched agencies to Ford. Even though she was making a six-figure salary as a commercial catalogue model, her parents insisted that she still get a minimum wage job on the weekends, working in a café, to know the value of a dollar. →

When she was 19, Ashley made her first appearance on the inside pages of American *Vogue* in a feature called 'Shop by Shape'. The following year she starred in a *Glamour* group portrait of curve models, called 'These Bodies Are Beautiful'. These sorts of editorial appearances were, however, rare and at times could be viewed as tokenistic bookings.

The first time Ashley publicly vocalized her frustrations with sizeism in the fashion industry came in 2010. She had starred in a television commercial for department store Lane Bryant – in the ad she paces around her apartment in her underwear, then, when she gets a calendar reminder to 'Meet Dan for lunch', she throws on only a trench coat and goes. Networks ABC and Fox refused to run it – the assumption was that it was 'too sexy'. When Ashley argued that the feedback was hypocritical and that the criticism wouldn't have happened to a size-zero model, she found herself booked to talk on America's biggest chat shows, *Jay Leno* and *The View*.

Ashley became nationally famous. She gained a few more campaigns with Levi's and Marina Rinaldi. Her following grew on social media.

In 2013, Ford shuttered its 'plus-size' division (it was later reinstated, in 2022). Ashley moved to IMG, and her career prospects changed almost instantly.

In the years that followed, she began to book covers for British *Elle, Sunday Times Style* and *Harper's Bazaar*. Then, in February 2016, came her historic *Sports Illustrated* swimsuit issue – Ashley was the first curvy model to book the cover.

Things were changing, certainly, but she still experienced regular rejection. Even when she starred on British *Vogue*'s January 2017 cover, the editor Alexandra Shulman wrote in her editor's letter, 'Sadly [some] houses flatly refused to lend us their clothes.'

Michael Kors was one of the first designers to back Ashley on the catwalk, when he booked her that spring for his show. After that, others followed – Fendi, Etro, Dolce & Gabbana.

It took 17 years from when she started on her career path for Ashley to finally be recognized as a legitimate supermodel, winning all the prestige covers and contracts available. She blazed a trail in a way that few others can claim – she never settled and was vocal, striving for more change at every stage on her route to success.

LIU **WEN**

//

27 January 1988

After a 20-hour train journey from her hometown, Yongzhou, Liu Wen arrived in Beijing in November 2006. She shared an apartment with two other aspiring models and began collecting some 2,000 fashion magazines, which she used as a reference library to educate herself on pose, photographers, designers and editors.

Growing up in China in the 1990s, Liu hadn't seen much Western fashion media. There were no mega-malls in her home province, and no magazines. But things were rapidly changing – the debut issue of *Vogue China* had just launched in 2005, appealing to a thriving new class of Chinese consumer with money to spend on fashion and cosmetics.

Liu's parents had encouraged her to enter the New Silk Road World modelling contest a year before, which was taking place near her home in Hunan. Even as a child, Liu was tall (she was 5 feet 6 inches by the time she was nine). She had lacked confidence, and her mother thought the experience might improve her posture.

Liu agreed to enter on account because the first prize was a laptop computer. She won the local round, but lost out to fellow Chinese model, Du Juan, when she went to the national finals in Sanya. Still, she was invited to work in Beijing and took the chance, assuming that modelling was a temporary job and that she might yet fulfil her ambitions to become a tour guide in Yongzhou. →

She began doing catalogue work, then editorials. High-art fashion shoots were a relatively new concept in Chinese publishing, and demand was picking up fast. Liu rose to prominence just as the country's new media outlets did.

Joseph Carle, then a creative director at Marie Claire International, spotted Liu at a fitting in late 2006. In her, he saw a model who might appeal to a truly global audience. In him, she found a mentor with experience in styling for both Eastern and Western markets.

Carle orchestrated Liu's debut cover of Chinese *Marie Claire* in September 2007, and she followed it up with covers for the Chinese editions of *Cosmopolitan, Vogue* and *Elle*.

Liu began working in Europe and walked in her debut catwalk show at Milan Fashion Week for Burberry in 2008. 'In my hometown, it was really hard to find high heels, so that first Milan Fashion Week I did was when I bought my first-ever heels,' she would tell *Marie Claire* in 2016. 'I didn't even know how to handle them. [Burberry designer] Christopher Bailey was really nice, he said, "We just want you to be a natural and feel like these clothes are yours."'

Liu's reputation as one of the most hardworking personalities in the industry was cemented a year later, when she was booked for 74 shows across the autumn 2009 catwalk shows. The record was higher than any other model in that season, and the most ever for a model of Asian descent.

She moved to New York and quickly mastered English the fun way – via Broadway shows, and by comparing Chinese and English versions of the Harry Potter books.

Once in America, her success story ignited and she was booked for advertising campaigns with Oscar de la Renta, DKNY and Calvin Klein, as well as numerous American *Vogue* editorials. She made *Forbes*'s best-paid models list thanks to deals with Victoria's Secret and Estée Lauder.

The biggest accolade, perhaps, came in March 2012, six years after she bought that train ticket to Beijing. *The New York Times* named her 'China's first bona fide supermodel'.

JOAN SMALLS

//

11 July 1988

Joan Smalls Rodriguez wasn't discovered by chance – she had a business plan. She presented it to her father at the age of 16, as she campaigned for him to lend her the money to travel to New York. Her goal was to attend open casting calls with some of the world's top modelling agencies.

Joan had grown up on the family's farm in Hatillo, Puerto Rico, but had decided at the age of 13 that she wanted to pursue modelling rather than becoming a vet. She was tall, and was diagnosed with scoliosis, which made her determined to stay fit and strong.

In 2000, the Ford agency held its annual global model-search competition at a resort in Puerto Rico. Joan was selected as the finalist for her home nation, competing for a prize contract worth $250,000. She ultimately lost out to Russia's Margarita Babina. But the experience shaped her; she has said that, in this moment, she realized she was representing not just herself, but her family and her community when she pursued this career.

She got a local agent and started to work, making $200 per fashion show – good, except that shows there were rare. Joan researched that New York's agencies would host regular open days; if she could just get to Manhattan she could knock on some doors. She proposed a schedule of appointments – she Googled addresses, times and directions – and showed it all to her father, explaining the return he might get on his plane-ticket investment if Joan and her sister were allowed to go and stay with their aunt in Queens.

The trip was signed off, and the tickets purchased. Joan arrived in New York and went to open calls with Women, IMG, Elite and others. She met with an agent who had seen her compete in Puerto Rico. He told her to straighten her teeth. →

"
I'M NOT IN THIS FOR THE FAME. I WANT TO BREAK BARRIERS.
"

'I said, "But I've seen other models with crooked teeth, why do I have to?"' she recalled in an interview with the *Evening Standard* in 2017. 'He said, "Well, Joan, because you're Black, and that is already going to be a difficulty in this industry."'

While most would be shaken by this interaction and the open acknowledgement of inherent racism within the fashion industry, Joan felt more determined than ever. She flew home, got Invisalign braces on her teeth and banked a psychology degree to keep her parents happy while she waited for her teeth to straighten up.

Her contact had moved to Elite and, true to his word, he signed her in 2007. Joan moved to Queens and spent the first year of her professional modelling career sleeping on an air mattress in her cousin's bedroom.

She first became a catalogue queen, working routinely for Neiman Marcus, Nordstrom and Macy's. She eventually got her own place and was comfortable – but not satisfied.

Taking fresh control of her career, she changed agents and signed with IMG to get the breakthrough she wanted. With her focus switched to the catwalk, it was designer Riccardo Tisci who first booked her exclusively for the Givenchy Haute Couture show in January 2010 – her eyebrows were bleached by makeup artist Pat McGrath.

Aged 21, Joan's image was instantly reshaped as a high fashion model. A month later, she booked 40 catwalk shows, including Prada, Louis Vuitton and Yves Saint Laurent. A history-making cosmetics campaign with Estée Lauder was hers.

American *Vogue* dubbed her the new 'It-girl' in its June issue. As street-style photography grew in popularity, she gained fans for her off-duty images, as much as for any prestige editorial. Editor André Leon Talley described her as a 'striking girl-next-door'. 'I'm not in this for the fame,' she told him. 'I want to break barriers.'

COCO **ROCHA**
//
10 September 1988

In the summer of 2006 on a rooftop above New York's Times Square, Coco Rocha was walking on warm tar. She was perfecting her runway stomp under the direction of Mac Folkes, an American football player who could strut in stilettos. The aim of the class? To walk with such purpose that your shoes would never get stuck.

Coco was preparing for her first full show season, but in the previous year had already gained a lot of experience as a model.

She was first discovered aged 14 at an Irish dancing contest in her hometown near Vancouver, Canada. The father of another competitor was Charles Stuart, an agent; he approached Coco and her mother.

Stuart became Coco's manager and helped her to set up some test shoots. He took her to a modelling convention, where international scouts were seeking regional talents to take to the next level. Coco got callbacks from every agency in attendance – and, ultimately, signed with Supreme in New York.

At 15, she was sent to Taipei and Singapore to build a portfolio, which it was hoped would qualify her to apply for a visa to live and work in the United States. She posed for dozens of catalogues, typically shooting 150 images a day, every day for two months. It was this crash course that taught her how to pose.

When she arrived back in New York, her agent sent her to a casting call with Steven Meisel. Meisel, famously, was amused by the range of poses that Coco threw for him. He offered her six months' exclusivity, working under his tutelage.

Meisel made an approved list of designers that he thought Coco should walk for, including Marc Jacobs, Gucci, Fendi and Christian Dior. As the show season began, word of 'the list' got out and other big brands vied to be green-lit too. →

Chanel, Spring/Summer 2007.

By the end of the September 2006 catwalk season, Meisel's launch plan had worked. She had featured in all the most important shows of the year, and her distinct walk had garnered attention from designers, but also from editors who could see that her angular, otherworldly beauty would also look unique on camera.

Meisel shot Coco in several memorable *Vogue Italia* concepts, as well as in his group composition for American *Vogue*'s May 2007 issue, starring 'the world's next top models'. Coco posed alongside Agyness Deyn, Caroline Trentini, Chanel Iman, Doutzen Kroes, Hilary Rhoda, Jessica Stam, Lily Donaldson, Raquel Zimmermann and Sasha Pivovarova – all wearing white shirts and ball skirts.

For her first solo American *Vogue* shoot, Coco headed to Maine with stylist Grace Coddington and photographer Arthur Elgort. Across 14 pages in the magazine, she modelled plaids, flannels and chunky knits as she posed with rusting ships, buoys and lobster traps.

With her profile now raised high in the realms of both editorial and catwalk modelling, it was only a matter of time before big advertising campaigns were also hers. Her character appealed to both the high end and the high street – with clients spanning Dior to GAP.

At a time when anonymous models were in favour, and uniqueness and personality were less in demand, Coco broke through. She understood the 'power of pose' like few others of her generation, according to *Vogue*, ensuring that her portraits are always dynamic. →

Q&A

with

COCO ROCHA

What are your memories of the day you were discovered?

My friends and I had just completed a dance set. It was 2003, and I was a tall, lanky teen who never caught the boys' attention. A man approached us with a stern expression. He asked 'Hey, have you ever considered modelling?' The question was so absurd that we all just burst into laughter. In our minds, models were these curvaceous bombshells, and certainly full-grown women. How could I, a pale, skinny 14-year-old girl, ever fit that mould? Needless to say, we all assumed he was either crazy, a pervert, or both. He persisted and reached out to my mom, who soon realized he was a legitimate agent with a concrete plan.

Your catwalk training was quite unique …

It felt like training with weights on, but if you could make it look effortless on that sticky tar surface, you could walk on anything. Not long after, I had my first casting with Versace. I didn't fit the typical model mould for them, and I could sense Donatella's scepticism about me. Brana Wolf, who was styling for Versace, picked up on Donatella's hesitancy and said, 'Just wait – watch her walk.' I gave it my all, delivering a powerful strut Mac [Folkes] would have been proud of. I remember Donatella nodding and saying, 'Alright, you can do the show.'

What inspired and informed the range of poses you are famously good at?

You might assume that Irish dance helped my modelling, but, in many ways, it had the opposite effect. Irish dancers are trained to maintain rigidity in their upper bodies, with the primary focus on intricate legwork. I had to shed many of those ingrained habits in order to move more fluidly for modelling. My posing style was truly shaped during my time in Asia. Casting sessions there involved models lining up in front of a panel of clients, akin to a real-life version of *American Idol*. In complete silence, we had to pose off against the model to our side for several minutes. It was brutal! If you stopped or ran out of ideas, you lost the job. Once you booked a job, you would then find yourself shooting catalogues, swiftly changing and posing in over 100 different looks a day, with just a few minutes between each shot. This meant you were striking tens of thousands of poses, day in and day out. Returning to North America, half a year later, I assumed this was how most models posed, but it really wasn't.

The story of Steven Meisel's 'list' became a legend in modelling. What was it like to have your career nurtured in this way?

At the time, I didn't fully comprehend the significance of having Steven Meisel personally oversee the initial year of my career. He essentially acted as my unofficial agent, and I wouldn't undertake any job without his feedback. During Fashion Month, by the time I reached Paris, all the major designers were eagerly enquiring if their names had made it onto the list. Looking back, it was extraordinary.

Was there a particular job that you felt changed everything for you?

My first shoot with Steven Meisel for *Vogue Italia*. On set that day were Edward Enninful styling, makeup artist Pat McGrath, and hair stylist Guido Palau. All are living legends in their respective fields. I shared the shoot with another model, Sasha Pivovarova, and at the end I confessed that I was unsure I'd ever have the opportunity to work with this extraordinary team again. After a long drag from her cigarette, she said, 'Don't worry, Coco, after today, you won't have to worry about finding work again.' She was absolutely right.

"

HEY, HAVE YOU EVER CONSIDERED MODELLING?' THE QUESTION WAS SO ABSURD THAT WE ALL BURST INTO LAUGHTER.

"

JOURDAN

JOURDAN
DUNN
//

3 August 1990

When Jourdan Dunn was first signed as a model, she set herself three goals. She wanted a *Vogue* cover, she wanted to be in the Victoria's Secret fashion show, and she wanted a beauty contract, specifically with Maybelline – at the time, three of the biggest accolades a supermodel could own.

'When I got [them], I was overwhelmed and crying with happiness and joy,' she later told website *Into the Gloss* of the moment when, in 2014, she had achieved her trinity, and would routinely spot herself on magazine stands and billboards all over the world. 'It's crazy because you start seeing it everywhere. I'll go to Boots [the pharmacy] and there's me; airport, there's me …'

Jourdan had been scouted aged 15, in London. She was in the Hammersmith branch of the high-street chain, Primark, messing around with a friend who was trying on sunglasses. An agent from Storm approached her and gave her a business card. She understood the association – Storm meant Kate Moss. She called her mother, a receptionist, and they both screamed. The following day, she went to the office and was signed.

At 6 feet tall – and seemingly all legs – Jourdan's natural starting place was the catwalk. During her debut show season in September 2007, she booked five shows – none of which were in her home city. Articulate, even as a teenager, she asked a reporter: 'London's not a white city. So why should our catwalks be so white?' →

Her observation caused reverberations – initially in the press, but then designers began to react. The following season, February 2008, Jourdan was booked exclusively by Prada, becoming the first Black model on the brand's Milan catwalk since Naomi Campbell in 1997.

Jourdan then fronted the 'Black issue' of *Vogue Italia* that summer. She was one of four cover stars – Naomi Campbell, Liya Kebede and Sessilee Lopez were the other three. The issue represented a watershed moment in global popular culture – in America, Barack Obama was on the verge of being elected. 'Though it may seem forced to link politics with fashion, history proves that the dominant aesthetic of any era can only reflect the mood of the times,' wrote Sarah Mower in *The Guardian*. Demand for the magazine was such that publisher Condé Nast printed an additional 40,000 copies.

Jourdan's name had gone global. At the September 2008 shows, she was booked by 75 brands, from Louis Vuitton to Valentino. Advertising with Topshop made her accessible, but she could also book Chanel couture. Titles like *Teen Vogue* were as likely to interview her as broadsheet newspapers – her profile was known to all audiences.

A year later, when Jourdan was 19, she walked the Jean Paul Gaultier catwalk at six months pregnant – the designer custom-made a corset to her measurements. She took maternity leave and returned with a double shoot in American *Vogue*'s September 2010 issue, shot by Peter Lindbergh and Steven Meisel.

Her openness, via social media and in formal interviews, was a rarity and her appeal went far beyond just her image. She was already a supermodel, years before she had met her own criteria.

PALOMA
ELSESSER
//

12 April 1992

PALOMA

Cosmetics contracts have long been treated like gold medals in modelling, awarded to only the most accomplished supers after years of runway, editorial and commercial success. Yet for Paloma Elsesser, it was a beauty advertisement that started her career.

Paloma was born in London and grew up in Los Angeles. Both of her parents were artists – her African American mother was a writer, her Chilean Swiss father a musician. While she was surrounded by creativity, she had no interest in becoming a model – fashion media wasn't a space that she had seen herself reflected in. Paloma completed a degree in psychology and literature at The New School in New York and worked as a waitress and a copywriter.

She was, however, inherently stylish and owned her unique look with confidence. It was her friend, the Australian stylist Stevie Dance, who encouraged her to visit a few modelling agencies to try out as a curve model, inspired by the success of stars like Crystal Renn and Sophie Dahl. Paloma was rejected, and moved on.

Instead, in 2015, she boarded a tour bus to manage her childhood friend, the rapper Earl Sweatshirt's, music tour. When they reached Philadelphia, she received an out-of-the-blue email from the renowned makeup artist Pat McGrath.

McGrath was looking for a fresh face to front her new cosmetics line and launch its debut product – a gold pigment. But rather than ask Naomi Campbell, Cindy Crawford or one of the famous faces she had been painting for decades, she had turned to Instagram and came across Paloma's profile. →

'That's pretty much the day that changed my life,' she told *The Daily Telegraph* in 2021. 'Because she was a person in a position of power who showed me that I could have a place in the industry. And she didn't want to change anything about me.'

The first batch of pigments sold out in six minutes – Paloma's selling power was proven, and McGrath called her 'my muse'.

She signed a modelling contract with the agency Muse and got to work. From the start Paloma was labelled a 'challenger' – a model who was out to change beauty ideals and drive inclusivity.

Her debut editorial shoots in 2015 were for *i-D* and *Wonderland*, where she was named 'best of the next'. Her early advertising assignments included Nike, H&M and Fenty Beauty. She was plastered on billboards, naked, as the face and body of Glossier's new Body Hero lotion.

For the next six years, Paloma was a highly successful model. She featured in British *Vogue*'s 2018 'New Frontiers' group cover and shot dozens of inside stories for American *Vogue*. Her career on the catwalk, though, was slower to progress, and she spoke often of her dismay that designers still resisted creating samples in any size beyond zero.

Things finally began to change (albeit slowly) in February 2020, when Paloma took a trio of top-bill bookings during fashion month. She walked in the shows for Fendi, Lanvin and Alexander McQueen – prestige clients on a level that no curvy model before her had reached.

The following year, she made it out of the inside pages of American *Vogue* and onto its cover. Annie Leibovitz photographed her in a soaked filmy Michael Kors dress that emphasized her curves. The tagline? 'Fashion's role model.'

'I've learned so much about myself and the next evolution of what I'd like my career to be,' she told the magazine. 'It's an immense honour even to be able to do this – but it also feels like something that should have existed long before I started.'

ADWOA

ADWOA **ABOAH**

//

18 May 1992

In the spring of 2015, Adwoa Aboah shaved off her hair. She had spontaneously decided to do it while on a trip to Los Angeles, consulting stylist Gareth Bromell. 'It was a kind of a f***-you to the industry, even if I wasn't conscious of that at the time,' she later told *The Guardian* in 2017. 'I didn't warn anyone.'

The choice, which would once have been deemed a huge risk for an established model, was instead celebrated by her agents and clients. It proved to be a career-making decision, as well as a life-affirming one – Adwoa shared her story with *Teen Vogue*, with the hope of encouraging girls globally to embrace their own beauty on their terms.

Adwoa had been working with some success as a model since 2008, juggling jobs around studying for a drama degree. As the daughter of British photographic agent Camilla Lowther and Ghanaian British location scout Charles Aboah, she grew up in London's Notting Hill surrounded by designers and photographers.

Alongside her childhood friend Cara Delevingne, she signed with the modelling agency Storm at 16. In November 2008, she made her debut in British *Vogue*'s 'New England' editorial, shot by David Mushegain, wearing brogues and a checked minidress. Her earliest catwalk shows were for London Fashion Week's young labels – Giles Deacon, Topshop and Simone Rocha. →

Adwoa has spoken openly about her struggles with addiction and depression throughout her teens and early twenties. It was her experience that inspired her to found the digital-community platform Gurls Talk in 2015, bringing important discussion about mental health onto the mainstream fashion industry's agenda.

After the haircut, Adwoa's modelling career gained fresh momentum. She was propelled from booking London-centric work – for titles such as *Love Magazine*, *Volt* and *Wonderland* – and began working more regularly with *Vogue*.

She made her *Vogue Italia* cover debut in December 2015, photographed by Tim Walker. The following spring, she walked in the international catwalk shows for the first time. She picked up high-profile advertising campaigns with Calvin Klein, Marc Jacobs and H&M.

While Adwoa had been a model for almost a decade, her real 'moment', as she would call it, happened in 2017.

That March, she joined Ashley Graham, Liu Wen, Imaan Hammam, Vittoria Ceretti, Gigi Hadid and Kendall Jenner for one of American *Vogue*'s culture-shifting group cover shoots. Photographed by Inez & Vinoodh on a beach in Malibu, and under the strapline 'the beauty revolution – no norm is the new norm', the image crystallized a long-overdue prioritisation of diversity in beauty.

Later that year, Adwoa made her British *Vogue* cover debut, this time appearing solo. Fronting the first issue under the new editorship of Edward Enninful, her image made headlines around the world, symbolising a new era at the magazine and Enninful's intention to make inclusivity the norm.

'In 2017, there is more than one way to be beautiful, and more than one way to be cool,' Adwoa told *The Guardian* in 2017. 'And when you put an image on the cover of *Vogue*, that means something that goes beyond fashion.'

KARLIE **KLOSS**
//

3 August 1992

KARLIE

Ahead of her runway debut, Karlie Kloss went to Target to buy her first pair of high heels. She was just 13 and was due to walk in the Threads4Hope charity catwalk show at her local mall in St Louis, Missouri.

Karlie had been shopping with her sisters when she was spotted by scouts and asked if she would audition for the event. Jeff and Mary Clarke, the couple behind local agency Mother Model Management, were the organizers – and intuitively spotted that Karlie could have potential beyond just this community project.

She wore sparkly silver leggings with a hooded dress and walked to Kanye West's 'Golddigger'. 'Something happened. For the first time I took on this other persona,' she later recalled in a Klossy YouTube video. 'I became another character.'

Karlie began working around her school schedule, mostly taking on jobs in Chicago. One particular story, titled 'Almost Famous', made the cover of *Chicago Scene* magazine and caught the attention of Elite in Chicago, then the New York office which signed her.

One of her first advertising assignments was for Abercrombie Kids, modelling T-shirts and denim shorts on the beach, photographed by Bruce Weber. It was Arthur Elgort who captured her first credited editorial – she showed off her childhood ballet training in a *Teen Vogue* profile, wearing leg warmers and posing at the barre. →

American *Vogue*, March 2010, photographer Arthur Elgort.

It is rare that a teen-market model should go on to find success as an adult – the two realms typically operate entirely separately. Yet Karlie by now had built a good rapport with top photographers and editors, so she graduated with ease.

At first, she juggled life between two worlds: high fashion, and high school. In September 2007, she enrolled for a new academic year on a Monday and walked her first New York Fashion Week show, an exclusive for Calvin Klein, on the Friday. Her life became a juxtaposition: Gucci shows and chemistry exams. She wore Dior to her prom.

By February 2008, work was intensifying. In a single season, she walked in 64 fashion shows, across New York, London, Milan and Paris. Scoring such a quantity of bookings had become a new measure of success – a way to spot the dominant model of the season.

Being taken seriously by designers meant Karlie could expose her range as a model – and, despite being an incredibly sweet person, she could really deliver an edge. Lee Alexander McQueen gave her one of her more extreme makeovers; in his 'Horn of Plenty' March 2009 show, she was eyebrowless, with blown-up oxblood lips.

This versatility and artistry all contributed to her achievements in advertising (her clients spanned Chloé, GAP, Dior beauty and Lola perfume by Marc Jacobs) and editorial too – by the age of 17 she was one of American *Vogue*'s most-booked models.

Becoming a 'multi-hyphenate' model then earned her an even wider audience – from selling cookies to promoting coding classes for girls, her sideline projects all added to her appeal. It was perfect timing – just as the world's biggest brands wanted to hire public personalities again.

C

A

R

A

CARA
DELEVINGNE
//

12 August 1992

With an older sister who was a model, and a godfather at the helm of *Vogue* publishing house Condé Nast, it was probably inevitable that Cara Delevingne should become a celebrity within the fashion industry.

But, in the early 2010s, there were plenty of British 'It-girls' having a go at some modelling. So, to become a reputable, world-renowned supermodel with career longevity, Cara required a different kind of energy – and a pair of highly expressive eyebrows.

Cara grew up in London's affluent Belgravia neighbourhood. Her parents, Charles and Pandora Delevingne, came from aristocratic families and were well-connected – able to choose author and media executive Sir Nicholas Coleridge and movie star Joan Collins as her godparents. On paper, she had all the glamorous associations a model could ever need.

Her first modelling assignment came at the age of 10 – the milliner Philip Treacy was being photographed by Bruce Weber for the pages of *Vogue Italia*. Cara, alongside Lady Eloise Anson, played dress-up in his sugary hats.

She pursued arts, music and drama at school, before signing with Sarah Doukas of Storm. Cara had been best friends with Doukas's daughter, Genevieve Garner, since childhood. →

'Sarah saw me when she came to our school and Gen introduced us,' Cara told *The Daily Telegraph* in 2011. 'I had never thought about modelling before, and it just happened.'

Cara began working as an e-commerce model, shooting five days a week on a contract for the fast-fashion website, ASOS. But when the Burberry designer Christopher Bailey saw her pictures, he decided she could be British modelling's next star.

Cara made her catwalk debut in Burberry's February 2011 show at London Fashion Week and was photographed for the season's advertising campaign by Mario Testino. In the March issue of American *Vogue*, she and Edie Campbell posed for Nick Knight in Burberry, illustrating a profile of Bailey.

Cara knew instinctively how to bring a picture to life – even her earliest shoots felt goofy and fresh. Sathoshi Saïkusa shot her for *Vogue Italia*, modelling yet more kooky hats. For *Tank* magazine, she faced off against her own 'twin', trying on two characters side by side.

It was her use of social media, though, that made Cara an innovator in her field. She starred in a 'world first' shoot conducted on Instagram, with Nick Knight in April 2012. She also knew how to use her social media accounts to raise her profile – a totally new concept at the time. Brands could see, with concrete data, how big Cara's audience was. And they could therefore measure the power she had to turn those people into potential customers.

2012 was a huge year for Cara, as she broke away from being Burberry's exclusive new face to walk in more than 60 catwalk shows. She appealed to every audience demographic, booking Chanel Haute Couture, Topshop, Louis Vuitton and Victoria's Secret.

Cara became a likeable rebel – from wearing onesies and eating McDonalds, to beatboxing for the paparazzi, her backstage antics became playful talking points in the tabloids.

In 2013, her numbers soared: 3 million Instagram followers (unheard of for a model at that time); 47 editorials, 14 of which were covers (6 of those were for *Vogue*); and 9 advertising campaigns, including Saint Laurent and DKNY.

Cara began to pursue an acting career as early as 2012, when she got a part in the film adaptation of *Anna Karenina*. By the time she starred on the cover of British *Vogue*'s January 2014 issue, she had made it clear that she intended to move on. In the accompanying feature, *Vogue* described her ultra-fast trajectory.

'In just over a year, and aged only 21, Cara Delevingne has turned into a model phenomenon,' writer Violet Henderson noted. '[She's] changed the fashion landscape forever.'

GIGI HADID
//

23 April 1995

There is a scene in the reality television series *The Real Housewives of Beverly Hills* that shows Yolanda Hadid accompanying her eldest daughter, Gigi, to one of her formative photoshoots. The year was 2012, Gigi was 18, and her mother was assessing her pictures on the photographer's monitor. 'She was bred for this,' her mother concludes.

It is true that Gigi had been raised as a model. She first posed for Baby Guess campaigns at the age of two – she grew up in front of photographer Kymberley Marciano's camera.

Born in Malibu, the daughter of Dutch former Ford model Yolanda and the Palestinian real-estate developer Mohamed Hadid, Gigi spent most of her free time playing volleyball and horse riding with her younger sister Bella and brother Anwar – both of whom would ultimately become models too.

But, as the eldest, Gigi went first, and her occasional appearances on her mother's show unwittingly charted the exact moments that her career as a supermodel took off. She moved to New York, decided not to pursue a degree in criminal psychology and signed with IMG Models in 2013. →

Gigi's arrival offered a new genre of model discovery story. She was a television celebrity with an established profile looking to be taken seriously as a high fashion model, rather than an unknown trying to make a name for themselves. In an industry that valued exclusivity, most jobs went to those who wouldn't distract from the clothes.

In many ways, Gigi has said, it was just as hard to become a supermodel this way around. She found many designers initially had snobbish perceptions about her background – she came with mainstream appeal and an enormous number of followers on social media. Designers, at that time, had no idea how valuable it could be to book a model with her own devoted fanbase.

Gigi broke through by accepting jobs almost on a stepping-stone route from commercial to high fashion brands. The former French *Vogue* editor Carine Roitfeld was one of the first to get behind her, commissioning Bruce Weber to photograph her for her artistic *CR Fashion Book*. Gigi made her entry at New York Fashion Week walking for Desigual and booked campaigns with Seafolly and Maybelline.

September 2014 was her first big international catwalk season; she walked for Marc Jacobs and Chanel. In 2015, she

balanced lucrative advertising assignments for Topshop and Tom Ford with yet more catwalk appearances for Versace, Balmain and Chanel couture. She also designed in collaboration with Tommy Hilfiger.

In a trio of Steven Meisel shoots, taken in 2015, her versatility as a model became apparent. Her feline, teal eyes popped next to a fistful of aquamarine rings on her debut *Vogue Italia* cover. She was ethereal, wearing a pink lace slip in W magazine. Then, for the 2015 Pirelli Calendar, she became a dominatrix in a glossy latex corset.

More *Vogue* covers followed. In March 2017, she fronted four international editions of the magazine at once: British, American, Chinese and the inaugural *Vogue Arabia*.

As Gigi's portfolio grew, so did her audience. The level of fame she had reached just a couple of years into her career was as great as most supermodels before her at their peak. She experienced Twiggy levels of hysteria wherever she went – the difference this time being that the phenomenon continued online and was trackable.

Never again would a designer book a model for a show or an advertising campaign without assessing how many social media followers they had. The Gigi effect would challenge the way that brands approached their marketing strategies going forward.

KENDALL
JENNER
//

3 November 1995

Almost every detail of Kendall Jenner's early modelling career was publicly documented and is available to watch online. Reality television cameras had trailed her since she was 11, when her family launched their globally successful show *Keeping Up with the Kardashians*. You can view the moment she first presented a scrapbook of pictures to her mother, the time she stumbled through her first runway coaching lesson, and the day she shot her first portfolio images after signing with Wilhelmina Models in 2009.

Being a teenage reality-TV star gave Kendall an unconventional start in the industry, and at times her background worked to her detriment. She came to fashion with her fame and following already made and, like her close friend Gigi Hadid, initially had to prove herself as a serious model, rather than as another famous 'It-girl'.

Her earliest assignments were for the teen market – campaigns for *Forever 21* and editorials for *Teen Vogue*. She walked in fashion shows at a local boutique, Smooch, which was owned by her elder half-sister Kourtney Kardashian. When she shot a lookbook of Sherri Hill prom dresses, she was asked to walk the runway publicly for the first time. Her celebrity siblings cheered her on from the front row.

In November 2013, when Kendall turned 18, she switched agencies to The Society and relaunched herself as a catwalk model. It was important, she has said, that her debut New York Fashion Week show presented her as she had never been seen before. →

"I WAS TRYING SO HARD TO BE TAKEN SERIOUSLY. "

Marc Jacobs did just that – in a uniform blunt bob wig, with her eyebrows bleached away, she blended seamlessly into the line-up of identikit beauties cast in the designer's autumn 2014 show. There were no family members in the audience, and there was no special treatment backstage.

'I was trying so hard to be taken seriously,' she later told American *Vogue*, of why she decided to make a name for herself as one of the most professional models to work with. 'This is what I want to do with my life. I had to prove that I could do it.'

Kendall's catwalk season progressed with bookings for Givenchy, Giles and Chanel. Her early covers, for artistic titles such as *Interview* and *Love* magazine rather than mass media, also helped to portray her as a mutable muse for designers to project their visions onto, rather than as a celebrity with a fixed image.

While cracking into the more exclusive realms of catwalk and editorial took a greater effort, advertising was an arena in which Kendall could excel. Commercial brands were already seeing the results of hiring 'Insta models' such as Cara Delevingne – supermodels with their own loyal followings. But when Kendall entered the ring, she did so with a fanbase larger than any before her.

Givenchy was one of the first to book her for campaigns. When Estée Lauder signed her as an ambassador in November 2014, citing her as 'fashion's new breakout star and social media sensation', Kendall already had 30 million followers. That number would eventually increase tenfold.

Kendall made her American *Vogue* cover debut in September 2016 – less than three years after her launch on the Marc Jacobs catwalk. The magazine dubbed her 'The Face that Launched a Billion Likes'. She was named the world's highest-paid model by *Forbes*, ousting Gisele Bündchen, who had topped the list annually since 2002.

'Now I feel like I'm a part of something,' she told *Vogue*. 'I feel I have accomplished something that is mine.'

BELLA **HADID**

//

9 October 1996

Good looks can run in a family. But while there have been a handful of successful sisters in the history of modelling (Dorian Leigh's sister Suzy Parker followed her to become a model then an actress, Janice Dickinson's sister Debbie shot French *Vogue* covers, and three out of Jerry Hall's four sisters modelled for a time) there has never been a pair of supermodel sisters on a par with the Hadids.

Bella Hadid has matched the success of her elder sister Gigi point for point, carving her own path while embracing the fact that they are related and occasionally modelling together.

Bella is 18 months younger, but of the two was perhaps the more determined to pursue modelling as a profession – this despite the fact that Gigi had modelled since she was a toddler.

By the time Bella was 18 years old and signed with IMG, she had seen Gigi's work taking off and actively wanted a career of her own. Her cameos in their mother's reality television show, *The Real Housewives of Beverly Hills,* are rare, but one scene shows her running through her test portfolio with her mother and sister, to get their feedback. →

Before Bella had designs on becoming a model, she was a competitive horse rider with ambitions to compete at the 2016 Olympics. Her family kept horses at their Malibu home and she had been riding since the age of two. As a teen, she competed internationally. In 2013, though, Bella was diagnosed with Lyme disease. Symptoms included chronic fatigue, and her dream was made impossible.

'That was my goal. If I'd had the chance to succeed in riding, I might not have modelled,' she recalled in a 2021 interview with American *Vogue*. 'I didn't know that I was going to get sick.'

Instead, she enrolled to study photography at Parsons School of Design in New York. Simultaneously, she was signed by IMG and was beginning to book some interesting shoots. She soon realized that she was learning more on set, from renowned photographers such as Mario Sorrenti, than she might from any college tutor.

Bella's first jobs included campaigns for Chrome Hearts, the Los Angeles accessories brand, and editorials for niche magazines *Jalouse*, *Out of Order* and *Grey*. In February 2015, Tom Ford cast her in her first New York Fashion Week show. In-book stories for *Glamour* and *Elle* followed, and she joined ensemble casts in Ralph Lauren and Balmain advertisements. American *Vogue* ran a story on 'sisters of', casting Bella alongside Kylie Jenner and Kate Moss's younger half-sister, Lottie.

Where many models with a society or family connection might have bailed out at this point, and settled for being a good model, Bella set her sights on becoming a supermodel in her own right. She understood that to be great, she needed experience, and she racked up dozens of credits during this time for young designers and lesser-known titles spanning *Wonderland*, *Allure* and *V* magazine.

The house of Christian Dior noticed her efforts, and she was offered a beauty advertising contract in May 2016. From there, her ascent quickened. She booked American *Elle*'s cover and her first Victoria's Secret show, as well as ready-to-wear and couture shows for brands from Chanel to Versace.

Because of her condition, she got tired more quickly than other models might – but as she spoke openly about her struggles, she was praised as an advocate for both mental and physical health in the modelling industry.

By the time Bella and Gigi shot their dual cover story for British *Vogue* in 2018, photographed by Steven Meisel, they were on an equal footing. The magazine compared and contrasted their achievements: blue-chip beauty contracts, jewellery advertising deals and catwalk appearances – they each had them all.

As a modern-day sister act, the Hadids were the most famous in the world.

HALIMA

HALIMA
ADEN
//

19 September 1997

In a line-up of blonde semi-finalists wearing sequinned mini dresses, Halima Aden made her mark on the fashion and beauty industries. She was competing in the 2016 Miss Minnesota USA pageant and was the first to do so wearing a hijab. For the contest's swimsuit round, she wore a black burkini.

Halima didn't win, but her confidence and charisma captured the attention of news networks all over America. Her consolation prize (or better than)? She was suddenly famous.

Halima grew up in St Cloud, Minnesota, from the age of seven, but had been born in the Kakuma Refugee Camp in Kenya. Her mother had fled the civil war in Somalia and raised Halima and her younger brother in a series of temporary homes, sometimes made with mud walls that could wash away in the rain.

Arriving in 'jeans town' in Minnesota in 2004, Halima grew up embracing the American tween fashion references of her generation (Miley Cyrus's *Hannah Montana* was a favourite). But she couldn't see anyone that looked like her being represented in the media. It hadn't occurred to her that she might be able to change that, until she was voted the first Muslim homecoming queen at her high school.

She entered the Miss USA contest for her home state, partly for the college scholarship opportunities, and partly to spread some joy within her community, as she had enjoyed the feedback from her homecoming experience. →

Following the pageant and the media coverage that came with it, the fashion editor Carine Roitfeld contacted Halima. She invited her to New York to shoot the cover of *CR Fashion Book* – Halima's first photoshoot ever. With Mario Sorrenti photographing, Roitfeld arranged for the supermodel Iman to conduct the corresponding interview.

With the shoot in the bank and ready to be released in the spring, Halima signed with agency IMG. In a four-hour-long meeting, her new agents asked questions about her preferences and requirements – a type of discussion that was new to both sides. Halima added a clause to her contract to ensure that she would never be asked to remove her hijab while working and stated that private changing facilities would be provided backstage. This, at the time, was revolutionary.

In February 2017, Halima made her debut on the catwalk. She walked first for Yeezy – rapper Kanye West's label – then Alberta Ferretti and Max Mara during Milan Fashion Week.

Advertising assignments with American Eagle, Fenty Beauty, Shiseido and Mac followed, as well as editorial cover shoots for *Elle*, *Glamour*, *Harper's Bazaar* and *Vogue Arabia*.

With such a strong, authoritative voice in the industry and a passionate social media fanbase, Halima was called a supermodel by the media in seemingly record time. *Harper's Bazaar Arabia* called her 'the face of hope'.

Certainly, she is one of the most effective changemakers the modelling industry has ever known. →

Max Mara, Autumn/Winter 2017.

Q&A

with

HALIMA ADEN

What originally made you want to enter the Miss Minnesota pageant?
Growing up, fashion definitely felt like a faraway world. Entering the pageant really stemmed from wanting to represent the young girls in my community – even the little girls in my own family that looked up to me. It's also a scholarship platform, so I thought it would be a great way to earn extra cash for school, sharpen my interview skills and get a bit of stage presence. Ultimately, though, it was that I was feeling that need for representation, even if it was on a small, local scale.

Your life changed overnight ...
Totally. To give you the context, I did the pageant on a weekend and by the Monday I had people reaching out wanting to book me. Rihanna's team DM'd me and flew me to LA to shoot for [her cosmetics brand] Fenty Beauty, which at that time was a secret project. Within that same week, I was also on a flight to New York for the first time to meet with [fashion editor] Carine Roitfeld. The editorial was meant to be a few pages inside her *CR Fashion Book*, but it became the cover. →

> ## " I DID THE PAGEANT ON A WEEKEND AND BY THE MONDAY I HAD PEOPLE REACHING OUT WANTING TO BOOK ME. "

How easy or difficult was it to then get an agent?

To be honest, I wasn't expecting to be signed because, at the time, there was just no such thing as a hijab-wearing model. When I first walked into [agency] IMG it was nerve-racking. The scout checked my height and, when it was 5 feet 5½ inches, she told me most models they have are 5 feet 9 inches and above. I walked out of that meeting and thought, 'Well, that bombed!' Then Ivan Bart [the late president of IMG] came running out of his office as I was leaving and said 'Halima, I'm so proud that we get to sign you.' I was like, 'Uh, did he just guarantee my spot? I think he just said, "Welcome to the family!"' I was so happy.

You set your own terms …

That contract wasn't something normal. I don't know how many newbie models will walk into IMG and say, 'Listen, I do want to model. But I'm going to live in Minnesota. I'm going to always travel with a female companion. And I want a hijab clause in my contract, that I won't ever remove my headscarf.' At that time, I was very strict – my neck always had to be covered and I was only wearing long dresses and long skirts. You won't see pictures of me in trousers. I was very specific because my mother, as an African, was telling me, 'No, no! You're not about to go dabbling in the fashion world without these requirements.'

You have achieved so many firsts in your career. Which moments stand out for you as game-changing?

Each moment, whether it's being featured in a major campaign or getting an amazing cover, has just been a profound reminder that there's so much positive impact to be had. I think the industry craves authenticity and I've learned that fashion will meet you where you stand. A monumental moment for me was meeting Adut Akech. We were in New York shooting a [group] cover for British *Vogue*, and it was the first time in the magazine's 102 year history that they had featured a woman wearing a hijab on the cover. Adut and I were talking, then I said, 'Where are you from?' We realized we were sharing this cover as two girls born in the same refugee camp, but who had grown up on two different continents [Halima in America, Adut in Australia]. That, to me, was just amazing.

ANOK **YAI**

//

20 December 1997

On 20 October 2017, Anok Yai had around 100 followers on Instagram. Within two days, she had more than 80,000.

While several supermodels before her had used Instagram to advance their profiles and careers, social media played a leading part in Anok's discovery story.

She was studying biochemistry at Plymouth State University, when she attended the homecoming weekend at Howard University in Washington DC with friends. The street-style photographer Steven Hall approached the 19-year-old, who was wearing denim shorts, and asked if he could snap her for his Instagram account @thesunk. He tagged Anok, his caption reading: 'Discovered a gem.'

Anok was born a refugee in Egypt, while her family awaited political asylum in the United States. The Yais had fled genocide in Sudan, and went first to Cairo, before arriving in New Hampshire in 2000. On arrival in America, Anok spent five years of her childhood in government housing while her parents worked long days. They valued education and encouraged her to pursue a career as a doctor.

While she was passionate about her studies, Anok had always been interested in fashion. She and her sister watched Tyra Banks's *America's Next Top Model* while growing up, and she has cited seeing a specific Naomi Campbell turn in a televised Victoria's Secret show in 2003 as a distinct memory. →

After Anok's picture went viral, model agents from New York began trying to get in touch – her phone 'blew up' she has said, with some calling her daily. Next Model Management's then-president Kyle Hagler was the one who ultimately signed her – the girl he had noticed when a friend shared pictures with him.

Just months later, in February 2018, Anok was on the catwalk. She opened Prada's autumn/winter show in an exclusive booking during Milan Fashion Week, making headlines due to the fact that no other Black woman had matched the feat of opening the show since Naomi Campbell in 1997. She shot a trio of advertising campaigns for the brand with photographer Willy Vanderperre while she was at it.

Editorials followed, first with *V* magazine, *Pop* and *Another*, then she joined an ensemble cast for a couture portfolio inside the pages of British *Vogue*. In July 2018, she got her debut cosmetics contract, with Estée Lauder, in seemingly record time.

By her sophomore season on the catwalk, Anok was seemingly everywhere. She booked all of the most influential shows, spanning Prada, Miu Miu, Saint Laurent, Chanel and Louis Vuitton.

Anok was a highly successful model. But it was her work ethic that defined her as one of the 'new supers', as declared by Models.com and one of the 'models changing an industry' according to American *Vogue*. She made a conscious effort to learn more about the business, rather than passively allowing managers to handle her contracts. Her approach is indicative of a new era of model moguls, stars who understand their personal audiences and how to market to them.

'I could have easily been a flash in the pan,' she told *Forbes* in 2021. 'And I'm sure that's what many were expecting, but right away I decided that I was going to do everything I could to become a powerhouse. Being a model means running a business, where essentially, I am the business.'

ADUT **AKECH**

//

25 December 1999

In a letter to her childhood self, penned for *Vogue Australia* in 2017, Adut Akech describes the expectations she placed on herself as a girl. 'I promised that I was going to make something out of myself,' she wrote. 'Something really good that would make people proud of me, especially my mother.'

Adut was just six years old when she arrived in Adelaide, South Australia. She had been born en route to Kakuma – the largest refugee site in Kenya, and coincidentally the same area as where Halima Aden's family had lived on their route from Somalia to the United States. Adut's family had fled the civil war in what is now South Sudan. Her auntie and sister were the first to get to Australia, with the rest of the family gaining their visas a few years later.

Adut's family made new roots – she first attended a specialist school, designed to teach English to refugees from all over the world, then moved into mainstream school. Her mother worked as a laundry supervisor, often doing 16-hour days. Her auntie sold her own clothing designs, and occasionally modelled in local shows. It was in one such show, at the Rundle Mall Plaza, that Adut first walked a community runway presentation, aged 13. Her interest in fashion was sparked. 'It was like fate,' she later told V magazine. 'After the show, I knew this was what I wanted to do for the rest of my life. I didn't know how far I'd get with modelling, but I wanted to give it my all.' →

Adut was approached several times in the following years by agents looking to sign her, however she prioritized her education. There was pressure from her extended family not to pursue the opportunity. At 16 though, with her mother's backing, she signed with Sydney's Chadwick Models and began working locally – modelling for the catalogue for department store David Jones, as well as walking 16 shows at Melbourne Fashion Week. She then signed internationally with Elite in Paris.

When the designer Anthony Vaccarello began his tenure as creative director at Saint Laurent, he sought some fresh faces to mark his new era. He booked Adut exclusively for the house's September 2016 show. It was Adut's Paris Fashion Week debut. She flew alone, for the first time in her life, to Europe.

Vaccarello booked her exclusively again for the following season and made Adut his spring advertising campaign star. To go so directly from being unknown, to being a poster girl for a storied Parisian house, was virtually unheard of at this time – unless perhaps you had arrived in the industry as a ready-made Instagram star. Naturally, editors and other designers paid attention and Adut shot creative editorials with Harley Weir for *i-D* and Janneke Van der Hagen for *Numéro*.

By the October 2017 round of shows, Adut walked for Saint Laurent again but, with her exclusive contract completed, she followed it up with appearances at Givenchy, Alexander McQueen and others. She became a Chanel bride (the finale model at any couture show), and a Valentino fragrance campaign girl. She charmed the establishment on her November 2017 Pirelli Calendar shoot – afterwards, Naomi Campbell called her a mentee. Edward Enninful called her his 'fashion daughter'.

By the spring of 2018, Adut was omnipresent in advertising for brands from Zara to Moschino, and appeared in fashion editorials for Australian, American and British *Vogue*. But via her impassioned speeches for the United Nations Refugee Agency, she was also gaining press for her activism work. *TIME*100 named her on its 'Next' list, and British *Vogue* called her a 'force for change'.

When, aged 19, Adut won Model of the Year at the British Fashion Awards, she had fronted five September *Vogue* magazine covers at the same time – this in an era where to book one would be considered a feat.

Her acceptance speech was distilled into an Instagram caption. 'Meet the South Sudanese refugee who comes from nothing, who just became your model of the year,' she wrote. 'I ******* did it!'

INDEX

Main entries in **bold** and illustrations in *italics*

PHOTO CREDITS

ABOUT THE AUTHOR

Caroline Leaper is the deputy fashion director at *The Telegraph* and regularly reports from the major fashion shows in Paris, London, Milan and New York. During her career she has also written for *Vogue*, *Elle*, *Marie Claire*, *InStyle* and *Glamour* and has interviewed stars including Naomi Campbell, Claudia Schiffer, Ashley Graham and Halima Aden.

ACKNOWLEDGEMENTS

I would like to thank every supermodel and super agent who said yes, and who kindly shared their stories and memories with me for this book. Thank you to Sophie Wise at Laurence King for your faith and enthusiasm, and to Sophie Hartley, Kieron Lewis and Jessica Spencer for bringing the project to life. To Bethan Holt, Lisa Armstrong and all my colleagues at *The Telegraph*, I'm so grateful for your support throughout. To my mum and dad, thank you for your endless love and guidance. Finally, to my husband Camron and daughter Eva – thank you for everything, you really are super.